Creative Writing
and
Self-Publishing
Your Way

ALSO BY M. J. SIMMS-MADDOX, PhD

The Priscilla Series:
Priscilla Engaging in the Game of Politics

Mystery in Harare: Priscilla's Journey into Southern Africa

Three Metal Pellets

Special Envoy 1: Priscilla Journeys into Arab Islamic Territory

The Mysterious Affair at the Met

Book Reviews by M. J. Simms-Maddox, PhD
Maqoma – The Legend of a Great Xhosa Warrior
Timothy J. Stapleton, 2016

Forewords by M. J. Simms-Maddox, PhD
Can't Complain – God Is Good to Me, My Story
Felecia Todeh Wesley, 2020

Creative Writing
and
Self-Publishing *Your Way*

A HANDBOOK

M. J. Simms-Maddox, PhD

M. J. Simms-Maddox, Inc. ~ Salisbury, NC US

Creative Writing *and* Self-Publishing Your Way

Copyright © 2022 by M. J. Simms-Maddox
All rights reserved.

Published by M. J. Simms-Maddox, Inc. P. O. Box 1966 Salisbury, NC 28145-1966 US
www.mjsimmsmaddoxinc.com (a.k.a., www.novelsbymj.com)

Library of Congress Control Number: 2022909646
ISBN: 978-1-7322406-8-1 hardback

Printed in the United States of America

Credits:

Pages 1-3 from *Their Eyes Were Watching God* by Zora Neale Hurston. Copyright (c) 1937 by Zora Neale Hurston. Renewed (c) 1965 by John C. Hurston and Joel Hurston. Used by permission of Little, Brown Book Group Limited, Carmelite House, 50 Victoria Embankment, London EC4Y ODZ.

Pages 1-3 from *Their Eyes Were Watching God* by Zora Neale Hurston. Copyright (c) 1937 by Zora Neale Hurston. Renewed (c) 1965 by John C. Hurston and Joel Hurston. Used by permission of HarperCollins Publishers.

From *Black Professional Women in Recent American Fiction* © 2004 Carmen Rose Marshall by permission of McFarland & Company, Inc., Box 611, Jefferson NC 28640. www.mcfarlandbooks.com.

Permission granted by the author-publisher, James P. Nettles, to use material from *Business Essentials for Writers: How to Make Money in an Ever-Changing Industry.* Charlotte: Author Essentials Publications, 2019.

Permission granted by the author, Elinettie K. Chabwera, to use material from *Writing Black Womanhood – Feminist Writing by Four Contemporary African and Black Diaspora Women Writers* © 2010, LAP Lambert Academic Publishing.

This handbook is an adaptation of presentations made by the author for professional development sessions at colleges and authors' conferences, including the African Literature Association and the Professional Woman Network. The author has also spoken about becoming a successful indie book author and publisher at events that empower women to improve their writing skills with the ultimate goal of publishing.

Disclaimer: Adherence to this step-by-step handbook does not guarantee that users will be successful in their writing and publishing endeavors.

"To be appreciated you must be read, and these things are invariably sought after with avidity."

Edgar Allan Poe, 1835

Who Should Consult This Handbook?

- ✓ Anyone who desires to write but has yet to put pen or pencil on paper or fingers on a keyboard.
- ✓ Anyone who writes but is unfamiliar with the publishing industry and desires to enter it.
- ✓ Anyone who has written some darn good narratives experiencing problems landing a literary agent and needs a shove to self-publish.

Figure 1. Girl Writing Clipart-Clipartion.com 19445

Aspiring authors, and even some accomplished authors, might find some of the content in this handbook somewhat daunting. But it took much time, effort, and money to learn what I write about on these pages. On the other hand, more widely published authors might find some of the material elementary. But this is, after all, a step-by-step approach to improving your writing, with the ultimate goal of publishing for authors who want to learn how to publish their work themselves.

Contents

Preface

After writing several book-length manuscripts and publishing four novels—one of which was recognized in the first-place category in an international book contest—and after speaking about becoming an independent book author and publisher at professional development sessions that empower women to improve their writing skills with the ultimate goal of publishing—I was encouraged to share some advice about my writing and publishing experiences: hence, this handbook.

Although there are many articles, books, videos, and webinars about writing and publishing, especially self-publishing, this handbook is a hands-on, step-by-step approach to improving your writing, with the ultimate goal of publishing.

And although there is no secret code or foolproof way to become a better writer and publish ultimately, all the writing guides and manuals on the market are of no use until you write that first word, sentence, or paragraph.

This handbook is divided into two parts. Part I – *Creative Writing – the Basics* is directed to emerging authors who desire to improve their creative writing skills. Toward that end, several standards are explored with corresponding literary works and exercises. The author also shares the five rules that she follows when she writes. These rules may or may not apply to your situation. The point is to establish a regimen that works best for you. Bonuses include discussions on the following:

- o   Trends in Hybrid, Indie, and Traditional Publishing
- o   Budgeting for Your Writing and Publishing Career
- o   Equipping Yourself with the Proper Tools
- o   Retaining a Competent Editor and Attorney
- o   Writing Query Letters
- o   Landing a Literary Agent
- o   Promoting and Selling Your Book(s).

The most critical step, however, is publishing, for which there are many sub-steps. Part II – *Self-Publishing Your Way* is directed to authors who desire to publish their work themselves. Instructions are provided in intricate detail, from obtaining a professional headshot, professional name, employer ID, incorporation, permission rights, copyright, ISBN, pricing, distributors, metadata, and BISACs to creating a domain, website, and a landing page, among other publishing essentials. Then there are the technical procedures to complete the process, most notably converting MS Word documents into book formats and ISO-validated digital and e-book files. After getting published—to bring attention to your books—authors must actively promote them.

Authors are encouraged to modify these rules and steps to suit their own situations in the final step.

Interwoven throughout this handbook are anecdotes, clipart, illustrations, photographs, and "words about...," such as "A Word about Literary Agents, Writing Query Letters, and ...," "A Word about Writing Standards for Fiction and Developing a Creed," and "A Word about Pricing." And although some of the clipart and the photographs were available for free online, I acknowledge each of my creative colleagues in the captions. But beware of "free downloads" because some are conditional. Is the use of the material for personal and educational purposes *or* commercial purposes? Read the fine print; licensing may be required. Some of the artwork in this publication was licensed through my subscription to Adobe Stock. Some of the photos of real people were taken by my spouse, Odinga Lawrence Maddox I, or me; professionals are credited on the copyright pages.

It occurred to me, late in this handbook's production, that many new writers might not be as skillful as I had assumed, which is why I composed this Preface. To be precise, my background lies in the social sciences—political science. So I adhere primarily to the APA style of writing (the *Publication Manual of the American Psychological Association*) and *The Chicago Manual of Style* (the *CMS*); but I am learning the MLA style (the *Modern Language Association*), essential for creative writing.

It has been quite difficult for me to transcend social science and adopt a more descriptive writing style—typical among practitioners in the humanities. Mine has been a world of research designs, literature reviews, and research methodologies, with such terminology as "hypotheses," "findings," "significant indicators," and "interval-level data." In addition, social scientists do not use personal pronouns; instead, they use impersonal labels such as "one," "this writer," "according to," and "the research shows."

Neither did I study creative writing in college. I have been told that my ability to write creatively is a "gift." Until I penned my first novel, *Priscilla Engaging in the Game of Politics*, I did not even know the elements of writing fiction; an editor first told me that I had written a novel. I share these insights with those of you— who—

as I once did—believe you cannot write poetry, fiction, or nonfiction because of your background, academic credentials, and so forth. Not so. Some of you have yet to put pen to paper or fingers on a keyboard. Consider joining the Association of Writers and Writing Program (AWP), "a national nonprofit literary organization for teachers and students," (https://www.awpwriter.org/awp_conference). And remember, regardless of your background, education, or life experiences, becoming a prolific writer takes effort, skills, and time—sometimes, a lifetime.

Therefore, you must first develop a skillset to write. For example, most prolific writers have developed their craft to the point that they produce high-quality work. How one defines such work depends on how authors apply several standards, such as practical word usage, conciseness, story structure, sentence syntax, subject-verb agreement, clarity, audience, layout, pagination, and storytelling and agency. Then there are the standards for creative writing: character development, especially of the protagonist, and other elements, such as the setting, storyline, voice, and structure (the stages in the story like the climax and a realistic ending). If you have already taken an English composition course and a creative writing course, none of this is new to you. Still, you might need to hone your skillset before starting your first significant manuscript.

Unfortunately, many wannabe authors will not comprehend any of this discourse until they begin writing. Even as I penned my first book, I did not know I was writing a novel, and the word "genre" was not even in my vocabulary. It was also an editor who told me that *Priscilla Engaging in the Game of Politics* was a coming-of-age story and that it was a political thriller, at that.

Writers must know their weaknesses. I often use the passive voice, and my incorrect word usage ticks off my editor. (Thank goodness for editors!) So even accomplished authors need to perfect their craft.

Writers must be mindful of the ever-changing technologies. Like many of my generation—Baby Boomers—I first learned to write in longhand and writing in longhand has stayed with me. I still write my initial thoughts and drafts on a legal pad, not on Sticky Notes or the OneNote on my computer. I used to transcribe my notes on a manual typewriter. Then came word processors, which I thought were the greatest invention ever! The IBM computers followed word processors and, later, the Apple Mac. But I survived, and although there is nothing as fulfilling and exhilarating as writing in longhand, I have come to appreciate all the features these electronic devices provide.

With advances in technology, writers must also learn the accompanying software, such as Microsoft Word and Adobe Acrobat Pro DC. This step-by-step approach assumes its users have a working knowledge of Microsoft Word and are somewhat familiar with Adobe Acrobat, but, just in case, a few necessary steps are outlined at different intervals in the sections about plotting the storyline and converting your manuscript into a book format and then a digital printing file. More knowledgeable writers may skip those sections and proceed to the next step.

If someone of my generation can transcend from the realm of the social sciences into that of the humanities—not to mention adapt to the ever-changing technologies—surely, some of the younger, new writers can.

Even so, success is relative. As an independent author and self-publisher, I believe there is more on the horizon—that is, that all authors can improve their craft better than readers regard our writing style today. It should be apparent that this author takes her writing seriously. But if the author does not believe in her work, why should anyone else?

The content, publication date, purpose, and title of this handbook—which some of my colleagues refer to as "an instruction manual" or "a textbook," whichever term you prefer—changed considerably throughout its production. Essentially, I wanted to produce a reference tool that enables writers to improve their writing skills and publish their work if that was their ultimate goal. In the long run, whether you publish your work yourself or retain a hybrid publisher, or search for a literary agent, there is nothing more empowering than knowing that you can publish your work yourself. Either way, I am reasonably sure something inside these pages will be advantageous in your quest to become an accomplished book author, maybe even an accomplished indie publisher!

Remember: what works best for you is the best way for you and no one else.

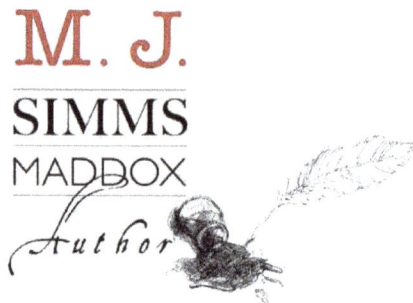

M. J.
SIMMS
MADDOX
Author

Acknowledgments

I am grateful to the Reverend Dr. Ada White Taylor for inspiring me to start writing professionally and Linda Ellis Eastman of the Professional Woman Network for setting me on the path to self-publishing. I am incredibly grateful to Fulbright Scholar P. Jane Splawn for introducing me to the African Literature Association and encouraging me to produce this handbook in the first place.

Much credit goes to Virginia Phiri of Zimbabwe Women Writers (herself an accomplished author) for the foreword to my first suspense-filled thriller (*Mystery in Harare: Priscilla's Journey into Southern Africa*) and for her unrelenting encouragement during the production of this handbook. Thanks also to Elinettie Chabwera, who chanced to self-publish for the first time based on a rough draft of this document, enabling me to make appropriate revisions before the book's publication.

I appreciate my editor, Lee Titus Elliott, for his work at the start of this publication. After that, so many other thoughts came to mind that I pretty much rewrote the document independently; hence, any errors are mine and mine alone.

Producing this handbook was no easy task. At times I felt as if I were writing a computer program—something I utterly detest. Even so, I must admit that I was invigorated as I progressed and completed this project.

Last but hardly least, I am incredibly grateful to Marie Umeh, Associate Professor Emerita-CUNY, UN Ambassador for African Women for Good Governance, and President of The Flora Nwapa Society, for reviewing this handbook and, of course, her impressive evaluation of it.

Figure 2. Creative Writing #2054966 at pppst.com. Clipart library.com/clipart/ 6TronBkc.htm. Phillip Martin Clipart Writing.

What Inspires You to Write?

To begin, put yourself in a specific frame of mind. Think about what inspires you even to want to write in the first place. I believe that most prolific writers receive inspiration from something, from someone, or from someplace.

In *The Young Writer at Work*, Jessie Rehder writes, "The disturbance which haunts a potential writer and draws [her] to pencil and paper is something which lies outside the range of books of instruction. It is so compelling, and so ill-defined, that philosophers of the past have called it a gift of the gods, and it is something which the writer must bring with [her]" (Rehder 1977, ix).[1] I agree.

The photo below is of the Indian Ocean off the Cape of Good Hope coast. How inspirational that is! People write for all sorts of reasons. My motivation to write fiction came through a recurring dream, and I have been writing ever since. The point is to start writing—regardless of what motivates you. https://youtu.be/CKffYNxX_wM

Let us turn our attention to the situation facing all authors in the early decades of the twenty-first century.

---

[1] Jessie Rehder, *The Young Writer at Work*, 1977.

Trending in Hybrid and Indie Book Publishing

As major publishing houses consolidate, merge, or dissolve, and, with over 1,000 books hitting the market daily—over 2 million annually—there is a growing presence of *hybrids* and independent publishers (*indies*) and corresponding availability of service providers. The difference between the traditional publishers, the hybrids, and the indies is that the traditional publishers pay an advance to the author and publish her work; they also handle the production, marketing, sales, distribution, et cetera. In so doing, once the book hits the market, the traditional publishers recoup their investment from a portion of the royalties from book sales.

Hybrid and indie publishers do not compensate the author with an advance; instead, the author covers the financial risks. The author pays the hybrid or the indie publisher to edit and proofread her manuscript, design the book, acquire the copyright, the ISBN, the price barcode, and everything else, up to the final book production. But a significant difference between hybrids and indies is that hybrid publishers must meet standards set forth by the Independent Book Publishers Association. So, authors need not worry about the quality of their end products.

Hybrids typically have experience with traditional publishing houses. Therefore, they are adept at publishing independently and can skillfully maneuver from the small to the medium-sized and more reputable publishers. As things stand, many aspiring authors are beginning to go this route, hoping to be picked up by one of the more reputable publishers sometime later. The choice is yours.

Authors might also opt to retain a hybrid or an indie for marketing services. Such is particularly the case for authors who are not adept at building platforms to garner readership and sales or for some other reason. But beware that royalties vary according to which publisher the author chooses.

Remember: this step-by-step approach is intended primarily for authors who desire to learn how to publish their work themselves. As such, all net profits accrue directly to them.

Yet if publishing your work yourself proves too taxing and your manuscript has yet to be accepted by a traditional publishing house, it might be best to retain a hybrid publisher. It is enough that authors spend excessive time, effort, and money researching and writing book-length manuscripts; it is another thing to then set about trying to publish them on their own.

Meanwhile, the list of hybrids, indies, and service providers is growing. Aspiring authors ought to take notice of this trend. See a shortlist below:

Apple	Featherproof Books
Audible	Feral House
Akashi Books	Forest Avenue Press
Amazon	Future Tense Books
Author House	George Braziller
Barnes & Noble Press	Google Play Books
Blackstone Publishing	iBooks
Blurb	IngramSpark
BOA Editions	Independent Publishers Group
BookBaby	Kindle Direct Publishing
Bowker	Kobo
C&R Press	New Pages
Catapult Books	Print-on-Demand Publishers, e.g.,
City Lights Publishers	Lulu.com, Publishers Graphics …
Coffee House Press	PublishDrive
Dorrance	Publishers Weekly, Poets & Writers,
Draft2Digital	The Writers' Chronicle, and Shelf
EPUB/MOBI	Awareness
Enchanted Lion Books	Scribd
Europa Editions	Smashwords, And More

> I am an indie author-publisher because the traditional publishing houses are not known for novels with contemporary professional African American women as protagonists. Learn more about this in "A Word about the Paucity of Novels about Contemporary Professional Black Women Protagonists with Agency: Possibilities for Black Women Authors and Other Fiction Writers" in Rule #4: "Your Writing Is Meant to Be Read."

The Future for Indie Authors - Publishers

The future looks great for indie authors who build substantial readership, remain proficient in the ever-changing technologies, and write excellent quality material. Before the COVID-19 pandemic, indies were publishing half of the 2.0 million books published annually—a significant indicator for a promising future! But during the pandemic, many more authors were added to those numbers.

Hopefully, I now have your attention.

Regardless of what one writes, serious authors follow a regimen to shore up their writing, so Part I begins with "A Word about Writing Standards for Fiction and Developing a Creed."

Figure 3. Gray and white textbook photo by David Iskander, unsplash.com

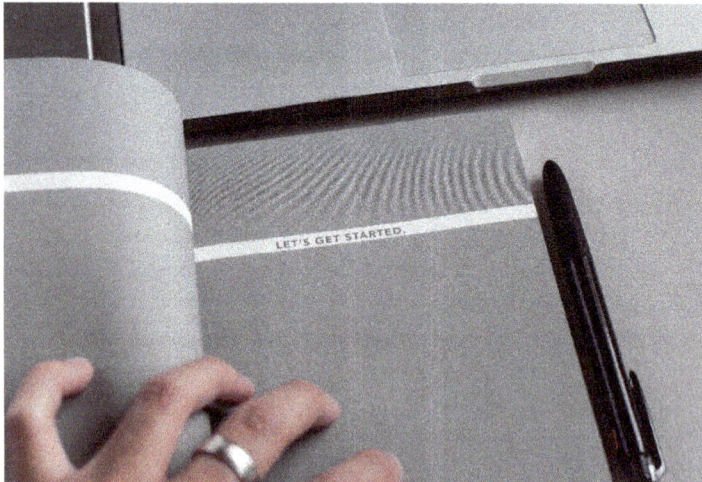

Part I:

Creative Writing

The Basics

A Word About Writing Standards for Fiction and Developing a Creed

Practitioners of any profession must adhere to standards, such as codes of ethical conduct and processes and methods. The same holds for fiction writers. Affiliate yourself with at least one statewide or national association to learn about proper behavior and writing standards, such as the African Literature Association, the North Carolina Writers' Network, and the Women's National Book Association.

In the Preface, I alluded to the many articles, books, and videos on writing fiction and self-publishing. Although written for college students some time ago, Jessie Rehder's *The Young Writer at Work* (1977) is an excellent resource for aspiring writers of any generation and is still highly regarded for the fundamentals necessary for writing good-quality fiction. I also recommend Edith Wharton's *The Writing of Fiction* (initially published in 1925), Alice LaPlante's *Method and Madness: The Making of a Story: A Guide to Writing Fiction* (2008), and Professor James Hynes's *Writing Great Fiction: Storytelling Tips & Techniques* (2014). Any or all of these books are excellent resources for anyone serious about creative writing.

Academics might find Helen Sword's *Air & Light & Time & Space: How Successful Academics Write* (2017) and Wendy Laura Belcher's *Writing Your Journal Article in Twelve Weeks: A Guide to Academic Publishing Success* (2008) more practical.

This handbook addresses a few of the standards for creative writing and provides corresponding examples in the literature. However, it would take one of the books mentioned above to cover all the criteria, not this handbook's purpose.

Aspiring authors might also find it advantageous to review the five rules comprising my writing regimen. At the core of my belief system are Rules #3 and #4: "Write about what you know—otherwise, conduct research, lots of it" and "Your writing is meant to be read." If I did not believe in either of these rules, I would never write. Developing a creed takes much time and effort, which can only come from experience.

All prolific authors follow some sort of regimen.

Rule #1: *Writing Is a Private Affair.*

> Avoid discussing your ideas and manuscripts with anyone other than your editor, not even with your family and friends.

This rule might seem strange, but you must protect your intellectual property. Your ideas and written material belong to you. Once you share any of this information with someone else—but you have not copyrighted it—you might very well lose your claim to it.

I almost always copyright my original manuscripts' rough drafts—with grammatical errors, loose structure, and the like. This way, I have something tangible to defend my claim.

Think about it. Why share your valuable ideas and work with anyone other than your editor, anyway?

Let me be clear: bouncing ideas off family members and close friends and colleagues is not the same as sharing your manuscript. If, for example, you come from a family of creative and supporting members, by all means, solicit their input. But many writers do not have such supporting circles.

And, if you have a supporting partner, someone whose opinion you value, go for it.

But it has been my experience that family members and friends contribute very little to my writing, hence my rule of thumb to keep my writing to myself.

Start creating a creed for your writing.

<u>Instructions:</u>
Think carefully about each rule. The point is to give serious attention to what works best for you.

Begin by noting what inspires you to write. Then, reexamine the rules that I follow and tweak them to suit your situation accordingly. On the other hand, you might prefer to create a set of rules of your own. For now, start with my first rule.

Rule #1: Writing Is a Private Affair.
If you agree with this rule, proceed to the second one.

If you disagree, describe your point of view about writing? Do you have a trusted confidante or an editor with whom you can share your creative writing experience? Be concise in your explanation about the suitability of this rule to your situation? (You might want to use a pencil so you can edit later.)

_____
_____
_____
_____
_____
_____
_____
_____
_____
_____
_____

Rule #2: *Successful Authors Write Every Day—Well, Almost Every Day.*

> If you cannot find a place suitable for writing at home, consider going to a library, a coffee house, or a hotel. Distractions—for example, cooking, housekeeping, work from the office, the ringing of the telephone, unexpected visitors at your door, or the presence of children and pets—often create excuses not to write.

Set aside time to write as often as possible. Once you develop the habit, it stays with you. Below are a few suggestions to aid you along the way:

- **When and where we write is an integral part of the writing process.** I write daily in my sunroom. Sometimes I write from early morning until late in the afternoon. Then I resume writing until an impressive show comes on PBS! However, unlike most people I know, I can write anywhere and under pretty much any circumstance. But when and where you write is your choice.

- **Sometimes, ideas come across your mind when you least expect them.** So, keep a pen and a pad or a recording device handy. Sometimes thoughts come to mind as you move about your home and office or socialize; jot them down. Do not tell yourself that you can wait until another time; note these thoughts now because you will lose them if you do not.

- **When writing, keep your Confidence Builders close by.** My dictionary, thesaurus, world atlas, and any other hard copy of a reference guide are always at my immediate disposal, even though I know that much of what I need is accessible in Microsoft Word and on the internet. On the other hand, some information on the internet is trendier than professional, such as definitions and word usage. Use your dictionary and thesaurus, not

25

Google. And let us not forget a reference book on creative writing, such as the *CMS* or *MLA*. All right, so I am old-school.

Continue developing your regimen for writing.

<u>Instructions</u>:

Begin this section by describing how often, when, and where you write. Consider talking to other writers to determine how often, when, and where they write. In so doing, you will have something else to aid in creating a rule that suits your situation.

Be mindful that writing is not a pastime for serious writers. Can you adopt this rule? Provide a detailed explanation. (You might want to use a pencil so you can edit.) Now, reexamine the second rule.

Rule #2: Successful Authors Write Every Day—Well, Almost Every Day. Suppose you agree with this rule. Proceed to the third one.

_____

_____

_____

_____

_____

_____

_____

_____

_____

_____

Rule #3: *Write about What You Know—Otherwise, Conduct Research, Lots of It.*

Start by writing about what you know. Then, research the unfamiliar and fact-check what you think you know. Consider interviewing experts, contacting a librarian, or performing extensive research on the internet. But when conducting research online, exercise caution in choosing sources. It takes a keen eye to discern reliable sources. Hint: search for "official" websites.

Use your skillset. Besides our chosen professions, most of us have at least one other talent or gift. I instinctively use my experiences as a political science professor to create backgrounds in my stories, such as descriptions of House and Senate chambers, cultures, and political systems. I also transfer some of my traits and life experiences to the protagonist in the Priscilla Series. See examples below:

> I am a preacher's kid (PK); Priscilla is a PK.
> I used to play the piano; Priscilla plays the piano.
> I am a professor of political science; so, too, is Priscilla.
> I have phobias, such as acrophobia, claustrophobia, and vertigo.
> So, too, does Priscilla.
> I once operated a public relations (PR) firm; Priscilla operates a
> PR firm.

Later in the series, I also transfer my writing career to Priscilla. Again, writing about what you know enriches the narrative.

Stretch yourself by writing about characters and subjects you do not like. Doing so creates balance, belief, and depth in your work.

Expounding on this rule and the next one brought out the professor in me. Recall that I did not study creative writing in college. So how did I learn? Apart from lessons here and there from my editors, I am self-taught. Curiosity also led me to inquire about writing from other authors. Some of them shared resources, such as the previously mentioned books on creative writing standards, whereas others recommended novels that reflect the creative writing essentials. If you are new to this craft, you, too, must learn the standards for writing fiction.

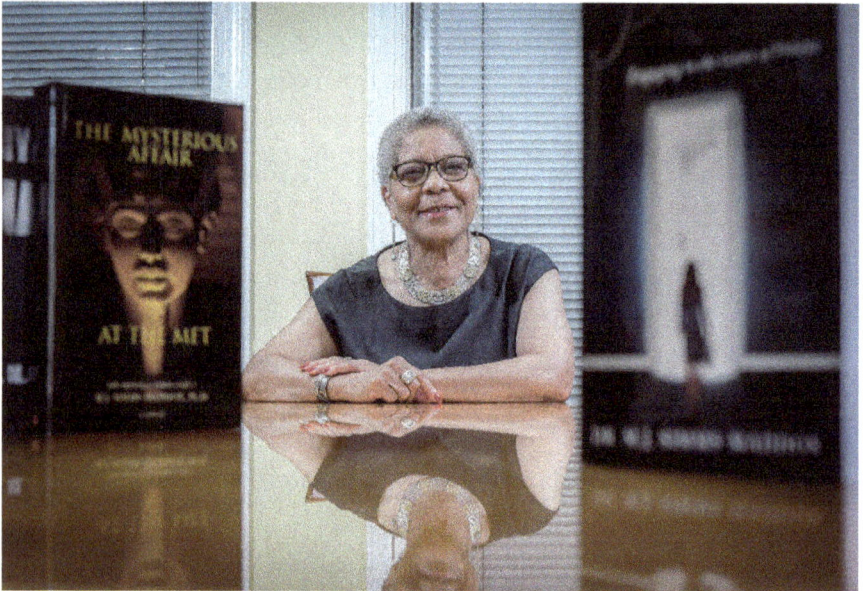

Shown above situated between her books is M. J. Simms-Maddox, PhD, author of this handbook and the creator and publisher of "the Priscilla Series". Author's photo by Sean Meyers Photography.

Continue creating your creed or regimen for writing.

<u>Instructions</u>:
It might be best to begin by noting whether you agree with this rule in its entirety. If not, refine the rule to fit your situation or develop your own.

Rule #3: Write about What You Know—Otherwise, Conduct Research, Lots of It.

Ever heard the expression, "Writers write about what they know?" This expression is not meant to be taken literally; instead, as a starting point. If you agree with this rule, proceed to the fourth one. Otherwise, continue with this exercise.

Have you read any books where the authors are known for writing about particular subjects, such as John Grisham, an attorney, and whose plots involve legal issues? J. R. R. Tolkien was a philologist, whereas Nelson DeMille has a military background. Prolific authors write about what they know and conduct a tremendous amount of research on the unfamiliar. Can you adopt this rule? Describe why or why not? (You might want to use a pencil so you can edit easily.)

_____

_____

_____

_____

_____

_____

_____

_____

Take a break from establishing your writing regimen and turn to the following section on "Creative Writing Standards". As you read each assignment, which of the rules mentioned above, if any, do or did those authors follow? Does their work read like they follow(ed) a relatively rigorous writing régime or write as a pastime?

Creative Writing Standards

Have you written your first story? If so, who is speaking? From whose point of view do you wish to draw in the reader? Does anything you write in the first pages cause readers to see, hear, smell, touch, or feel what is happening? Does the *first-person narrator* tell your story? If so, "I" is the focus throughout the narrative.

> **Homework.** Go to a public library and obtain copies of Ralph Ellison's *Invisible Man*, Chimamanda Ngozi Adichie's *AMERICANAH*, Nelson DeMille's *Up Country*, Zora Neale Hurston's *Their Eyes Were Watching God*, and J. R. R. Tolkien's *The Lord of the Rings – The Fellowship of the Ring*. Read the opening passage in the first four novels and pages 370-371 in *The Fellowship of the Ring* because this next section assumes your familiarity with this material.

One of the most compelling openings in a novel narrated in the first person is found in the first sentence of *Invisible Man*. Initially published in 1952, the author forces readers to question what it means to be invisible. Do you sense what he feels like knowing that people do not see him? Or is it that people refuse to see him? If at all, do you realize that the main character is a Black man? Can you even imagine how he feels? The universality of the subject comes to the fore in that anyone who has ever felt isolated or discriminated against for whatever reason can relate to this character. Does the "I" draw you into the story?

Ralph Ellison wrote about what he knew: life as a young Black man growing up in the racially segregated South in the early twentieth century and experiencing incredible ordeals trying to make a go of it, all of which, ultimately, causes him to reflect on his life as an invisible man (Ellison, 1990). Among his many honors, Ellison also won the National Book Award and the Russwurm Award.

Some sixty-odd years later, Chimamanda Ngozi Adichie evokes the reader's sensory perceptions while employing the *third-person narrator* to introduce her main character in AMERICANAH (2013). The narrator speaks as "she" or "her," or by her name. This author, who is Nigerian, brings the main character to life, simultaneously creating a place or setting—a province—from the very start. (I reference the author's nationality for you to know that creative writing standards are universal.) Even if you have never been to Princeton, you can sense how the university campus and the surrounding community smell. Readers can see the affluent dwellers going about their daily lives and more, as the main character shows you what it is like being the only one of her kind in their midst.

Adichie does what Rehder (1977) describes as wearing your characters' clothes and feeling by proxy with the people you create. "Beyond that, you will be moving with them through the fictional territory that is their home, instilling in your readers the spirit of that place. You will be establishing your *province*" (13).

A winner of the National Book Critics Circle award, Adichie writes about what she knows, including her family, friends, and acquaintances in Nigeria, Britain, the United States, and other places. But to write such a story, albeit fiction, one must be comfortable with herself, such as both Adichie and Ellison, who disclose pretty much all aspects of their lives and put their feelings into words. Can you write like that? It might take a while, but you, too, can hone your craft to the point of creating your own writing style, especially if you start with what you know.

We turn now to another celebrated novelist. Like Ellison, Nelson DeMille is very good at constructing characters speaking in the first person and setting up opening scenes that draw readers into his stories. In the opening scene in *Up Country* (DeMille 2002), readers can almost see the message that he uses to introduce the main character—who then takes over and tells readers what is in the message, what else happens in the short run, where he is, even what the weather is.

DeMille has created a living character and has placed him in a believable setting, landscape, or locale—whichever term you prefer. He is the focal point, like a captain steering a ship. Readers are eager to find out more about him and what happens next. And they want to meet the other characters and learn how they fit into the impending conundrum.

The author's note in the novel's front and final pages informs readers about his research writing *Up Country*. If a noted novelist like Nelson DeMille performs research to write his books, you and I must surely do likewise.

Yet another renowned author, Zora Neale Hurston, has quite a different writing style than Adichie's, DeMille's, or Ellison's. Hurston's *Their Eyes Were Watching God* was initially published in 1937. Her novel begins from the *omniscient* perspective, one benchmark or point of view used chiefly in fiction, especially novels. Then she switches to the *third-person point of view*. Then again, near the end of the first scene, yet another voice is heard, that of the story's narrator expanding the protagonist's voice into a *communal mode*, or communal point of view. (See Mary Helen Washington's explanation about this and more in her foreword to the book's 1990 edition (Hurston 1990, xiv)). For now, let us examine the opening passage of Hurston's novel more closely.

> *Ships at a distance have every man's wish on board. For some they* come in with the tide. For others they sail forever on the horizon, never out of sight, never landing until the Watcher turns his eyes away in resignation, his dreams mocked to death by Time. That is the life of men.
>
> Now, women forget all those things they don't want to remember, and remember everything they don't want to forget. The dream is the truth. Then they act and do things accordingly.
>
> So the beginning of this was a woman and she had come back from burying the dead. Not the dead of sick and ailing with friends at the pillow and the feet. She had come back from the sodden and the bloated; the sudden dead, their eyes flung wide open in judgment.
>
> The people all saw her come because it was sundown. The sun was gone, but he had left his footprints in the sky. It was the time for sitting on porches beside the road. It was the time to hear things and talk. These sitters had been tongueless, earless, eyeless conveniences all day long. Mules and other brutes had occupied their skins. But now, the sun and the bossman were gone, so the skins felt powerful and human. They became lords of sounds and lesser things. They passed nations through their mouths. They sat in judgment.
>
> Seeing the woman as she was made them remember the envy they had stored up from other times. So they chewed up the back parts of their minds and swallowed with relish. They made burning statements with questions, and killing tools out

of laughs. It was mass cruelty. A mood come alive. Words walking without masters; walking altogether like harmony in a song.

"What she doin coming back here in dem overhalls? Can't she find no dress to put on?—Where's dat blue satin dress she left here in?—Where all dat money her husband took and died and left her?—What dat ole forty year ole 'oman doin' wid her hair swingin' down her back lak some young gal?—Where she left dat young lad of a boy she went off here wid?—Thought she was going to marry?—Where he left *her*?—What he done wid all her money?—Betcha he off wid some gal so young she ain't even got no hairs—Why she don't stay in her class?—"

When she got to where they were she turned her face on the bander log and spoke. They scrambled a noisy "good evenin'" and left their mouths setting open and their ears full of hope. Her speech was pleasant enough, but she kept walking straight on to her gate. The porch couldn't talk for looking.

The men noticed her firm buttocks like she had grape fruits in her hip pockets; the great rope of black hair swinging to her waist and unraveling in the wind like a plume; then her pugnacious breasts trying to bore holes in her shirt. They, the men, were saving with the mind what they lost with the eye. The women took the faded shirt and muddy overalls and laid them away for remembrance. It was a weapon against her strength and if it turned out of no significance, still it was a hope that she might fall to their level some day.

But nobody moved, nobody spoke, nobody even thought to swallow spit until after her gate slammed behind her.

Pearl Stone opened her mouth and laughed real hard because she didn't know what else to do. She fell all over Mrs. Sumpkins while she laughed. Mrs. Sumpkins snorted violently and sucked her teeth.

"Humph! Y'll let her worry yuh. You ain't like me. Ah ain't got her to study 'bout. If she ain't got manners enough to stop and let folks know how she been makin' out, let her g'wan!"

"She ain't even worth talkin' after," Lulu Moss drawled through her nose. "She sits high, but she looks low. Dat's what Ah say 'bout dese ole women runnin' after young boys."

Pheoby Watson hitched her rocking chair forward before she spoke. "Well, nobody don't know if it's anything to tell or not. Me, Ah'm her best friend, and *Ah* don't know."

"Maybe us don't know into things lak you do, but we all know how she went 'way from here and us sho seen her come bak. 'Tain't no use in your tryin' to cloak no ole woman lak Janie Starks, Pheoby, friend or no friend."

"At dat she ain't so ole as some of y'all dat's talking."

"She's way past forty to my knowledge, Pheoby."

"No more'n forty at de outside."

"She's 'way too old for a boy like Tea Cake."

"Tea Cake ain't been no boy for some time. He's round thirty his ownself."

"Don't keer what it was, she could stop and say a few words with us. She act like we done done something to her," Pearl Stone complained. "She de one been doin' wrong."

"You mean, you mad' cause she didn't stop and tell us all her business. Anyhow, what you ever know her to do so bad as y'all make out? The worst thing Ah ever knowed her to do was taking a few years offa her age and dat ain't never harmed nobody. Y'all makes me tired. De way you talkin' you'd think de folks in dis town didn't do nothin' in de bed 'cept praise de Lawd. You have to 'scuse me, 'cause Ah'm bound to go take her some supper." Pheoby stood up sharply (Hurston 1990, 1-3).[2]

More about DeMille and Hurston

Can you think of anything that endears you to a particular author? What do you know about your favorite authors? Both DeMille and Hurston craft vivid, realistic settings. But why do the characters in Hurston's novel speak what is commonly referred to as "broken English"? Why does one author use the first-person voice while the other, the third person? When did DeMille write *Up Country*? When did

---

[2] Reprinted by permission of HarperCollins Publishers and Little, Brown Book Group, Ltd.

Hurston write *Their Eyes Were Watching God*? Let us take a closer look at the backgrounds of these two authors.

A native New Yorker, Nelson DeMille is a white man. He was born in 1943, grew up on Long Island, and studied history and political science in college. Anyone who has read his work knows the author was an officer in the U.S. Army and served active duty in the Vietnam War, a perspective from which he writes admirably. In his middle thirties, he published a fascinating bestseller *By the Rivers of Babylon* (1978). And there were comparably few, if any, questions about the credibility of the book's subject matter—a failed peace mission between the Arabs and Israelis— a stark contrast to the reception of Hurston's *Their Eyes Were Watching God.*

Like DeMille, Hurston was already an accomplished author in her middle thirties. It would, however, be decades later, and after she died in 1960 before *Their Eyes Were Watching God* would attain worldwide acclaim. Why was that?

Hurston, a native Floridian, was a Black woman. Born in 1891, she was raised in the only incorporated all-Black town in America—Eatonville, Florida. Her father served as the town's alderman and three times as its mayor. Hurston studied folklore and anthropology in college in the early twentieth century, whereas DeMille studied history and political science during the third quarter.

However, in the mid-to-late 1930s, the traditionally white, male-dominated literary establishment refused to accept Hurston's early work, especially *Their Eyes Were Watching God*. Most of the critics in the literary establishment, including Black male literary critics, gave the novel poor reviews. Black authors, like Richard Wright, Ralph Ellison, and the poet Langston Hughes, wrote in the protest tradition. An independent Black woman author, Hurston did not follow suit.

Why is that significant? For one thing, Hurston's portrayal of Janie Crawford—a Black female (more precisely, a mulatto) heroine in the late 1930s—made the story "unbelievable." Nor did many readers believe the veracity of an all-Black incorporated town, and certainly not one that Black people governed in America.

Interestingly also, Margaret Mitchell's *Gone with the Wind,* published in 1936, portrays Scarlett O'Hara finding love as she struggles to survive at her beloved Tara outside Atlanta, Georgia, amid the devastation of the American Civil War.

Likewise, in Eatonville, Florida, Janie Crawford finds love at the end of the Great Depression as she searches for her identity. Although both books feature romance and tragedy, most American readers, at the time—seventy-odd years after the American Civil War—still could not fathom a Black romance novel, not even an identity quest—the sheer irony of it all.

As writers, we must be cognizant of the context of our work. Stay true to the context, no matter the criticism. Thank goodness Hurston did not allow others' perceptions about her work to cloud her judgment. She wrote about what she knew, and she knew the Eatonville environment well. She had lived there and studied the culture as a folklorist and an anthropologist. When the literary critics and the marketplace finally came around to accepting Hurston's work, the *Saturday Review* noted: "*Their Eyes* belongs in the same category with [the works of] William Faulkner, F. Scott Fitzgerald, and Ernest Hemingway, that of enduring American literature." June Jordan of *Black World* rendered an equally impressive review: "The prototypical Black novel of affirmation: it is the most successful, convincing, and exemplary novel of Black love that we have. Period."

> A word of *caution*: although fiction is based on a kernel of truth, to avoid libel suits, change the names of events, people, and places, and embellish them. In addition, create as much as your imagination reveals to you.

We conclude this section on writing about what you know and conducting research about that with which you are unfamiliar with a look at J. R. R. Tolkien's work. Tolkien and his contemporaries—C. S. Lewis and George McDonald—were groundbreakers in fantasy writing.

Did you know that *before* Tolkien wrote *The Hobbit* and *The Lord of the Rings* trilogy, he'd had a successful career as a philologist? As such, his early works provided the foundation for his creation of what the world now knows as "Middle Earth."

Tolkien was born in Bloemfontein, South Africa, in 1892. He served in World War I, had a distinguished academic career, and was recognized as one of the world's finest philologists. He also served as a professor of Anglo-Saxon at Oxford, a fellow of Pembroke College, and a fellow of Merton College. Tolkien published *The Hobbit* in 1937, the same year that Hurston published *Their Eyes Were Watching God.* Yet, as fantasy, his novel is different than either Hurston's, DeMille's, Adichie's, or Ellison's, for that matter.

Even though his work as a professor and the onslaught of World War II adversely affected his writing, he persevered. Then, after he finished *The Lord of the Rings* trilogy, he had to start over and rewrite it backward. Imagine his fingers, one by one, typing that lengthy series on an old-fashioned typewriter—because he could not afford a typist. And correction tape and fluid had yet to be invented. Try also imagining how he must have contended with the early mixed reviews: some readers found the series incredible, whereas others wanted to know more about those people called "hobbits." Tolkien, however, went with his own thinking. His knowledge of ancient cultures, language, and literature, plays prominently in his writing. You, too, might find yourself in a comparable situation. But it is you, and you alone, who must determine whether to yield to criticism if any.

Tolkien published *The Lord of the Rings* trilogy in 1954 and 1955. But it would be a decade later, when the trilogy achieved acclaim and, man alive, did it! Then came the movie version at the turn of the twenty-first century, during which time book sales for the trilogy skyrocketed.

Let us now examine the passage from your homework from *The Fellowship of the Ring* in which the protagonist's entourage makes its way across that frightening bridge. Do you agree that the *omniscient* point of view intensifies the scene more than any other perspective—for example, the first person, the third person, or the communal? Let us review this passage more closely.

Like the first-person narrator, the third person can only see, hear, touch, smell, and feel what she experiences, not the big picture, an advantage of the omniscient perspective. Nor can the first-person (Frodo) or the third-person narrator convey to readers what someone else is thinking, such as the companion (Sam), who is with the protagonist; his companion has serious thoughts about their situation, which we learn from the omniscient perspective. Only the omniscient point of view can effectively convey to the reader what the main character, his companion, and all the other characters are doing and what they are thinking, not to mention what is happening with the characters that are somewhere other than that bridge. This particular perspective is functional because so much is happening to make it possible to destroy the ring. Therefore, the main character cannot realistically narrate this story with the omniscient narrator's seemingly all-knowing, commanding, and roaring voice.

I hope that writers at all levels and circumstances are enlightened. Not everyone who desires to write has the privileges of time, money, and other resources—not even a typist or correction fluid, not to mention a computer. Nor does the publishing industry or the marketplace accept certain work, particularly material that falls outside the established norms. In Tolkien's case, the work was a fantasy series. For Hurston, it was a romance novel about a young woman who happened to be Black, searching for her identity. Yet both Hurston and Tolkien somehow found ways to continue writing; so, too, must you and I.

Do you sense that writing is or was a full-time endeavor of Ellison's, Adichie's, DeMille's, Hurston's, and Tolkien's? If you have read at least one of their books, was it not evident that these authors spent lots of time, energy, and sometimes money researching their subject? Was it apparent that they adhered to rigorous writing routines? If you are serious about your writing career, so, too, must you.

A Writing Exercise

Compose a short story about three people seeking a hotel suite in 2050. In so doing, review the opening scene in Adichie's AMERICANAH where the protagonist draws the reader into the Princeton community while showing us who she is. Notice how the protagonist in DeMille's *Up Country* describes himself and shows us the setting; he serves as the first-person narrator. Practice writing from different points of view. Switch from the first person to the third person. Also, consider Tolkien's scene at the Bridge of Khazad-Dûm, in which the omniscient point of view speaks. Which point of view works best for you? Rehder (1977) calls this type of exercise "Visualizing a Scene" (38).

Recall how DeMille, Hurston, and Tolkien all use the dialects and the terminology spoken by the people about whom they write. For example, DeMille uses many terms involving the military and espionage, whereas Hurston employs the dialect spoken by the Eatonville residents during the 1930s.

"Show" scenes without "telling" the reader about them. Hurston's depiction of the porch scene in *Their Eyes Were Watching God* is an excellent example of bringing the locale to life, not to mention Adichie's Princeton province. Let us not forget that frightening scene that Tolkien created at the Bridge of Khazad-Dûm.

Lastly, in showing a scene, try to incorporate some "conflict," a topic we will cover shortly.

Some Extra Credit

Read Paula Hawkins' *The Girl on the Train* (2015). A journalist by occupation, this is her first novel. How would you categorize this novel? A psychological thriller, Hitchcock style? Who is narrating the story? Is someone rendering an account on behalf of the others? Does the omniscient come into play? Can you write like this? Now, do you see what I meant when I wrote in the Preface that one's background does not preclude her from writing fiction or pursuing her life's passion?

Hopefully, your confidence builds as you learn more about crafting your story. We turn now to the fourth rule in my writing regimen.

Rule #4: *Your Writing Is Meant to Be Read.*

Long after our generation expires, would it not be wonderful if some of our work was uncovered at a time long into the future and used to substantiate or invalidate issues of concern to society? Think about it. The discovery of the Dead Sea Scrolls comes to mind. And what about *The Diary of Anne Frank*? What if someone far into the future wants to know how people coped during the COVID-19 pandemic during the early twenty-first century? I think you get my point.

Figure 4. Edgar Allan Poe
Adobe Stock_957-85410

I write first because I want someone to read my books and be informed, entertained, and inspired.

I write because I want to add my voice to the literary canon. Just as scholars reference Jewish historian Josephus Flavius's accounts of the Jews from early Biblical times to the outbreak of the revolution of AD 66 and Jewish life during NT times, and, lest we forget Greek historian Herodotus' accounts of the Persians c. 484-425/413 BCE, let it be recorded that M. J. Simms-Maddox's novels provide a realistic version of the culture of African Americans from the mid-twentieth to the early twenty-first century.

Another reason that I write is that it is therapeutic.

Mostly though, like Edgar Allan Poe, I believe, "To be appreciated you must be read…."

Continue developing your creed or regimen for writing.

<u>Instructions</u>:
Reexamine the fourth rule as you continue thinking about what works best for you. Perhaps you might wish to reconsider why you write in the first place.

Rule #4: Your Writing Is Meant to Be Read.

What are your views about this rule? If you agree, continue to the fifth one. Otherwise, note the reasons for your disagreement in the space provided below. (You might want to use a pencil so you can edit easily.)

_____

_____

_____

_____

_____

_____

_____

_____

_____

_____

Now, let us create a template and begin plotting the storyline for your book, after which we will conclude this section with my fifth and final rule about writing.

Plotting the Storyline and More Creative Writing Techniques

First, Set Up a Framework, or a Working Template, for Your Manuscript in Microsoft Word.

- If you are just getting started, choose your trim size. Will your book measure five inches by eight inches (5" x 8") or six inches by nine inches (6" x 9")? These are the industry standards.
- Single-space the Front Matter, such as the copyright page.
- Double-space the text of your story.
- Use an eye-friendly font, such as twelve-point (12') Times New Roman or ten to eleven-point (11') Minion Pro Med. (Minion Pro Med and Alga are the primary fonts in this handbook, along with Candara for sub-headings.)
- Use your initial ideas to create sections, scenes, or chapters.
- Then, make page breaks to separate the chapters.

> Besides saving your manuscript on your hard drive, save it on a disk or separate storage or backup device, such as the cloud, and then write a note to remind yourself where you put it, for computers may crash or otherwise malfunction.

In a Separate File, Create a Profile for Each Character.

While creating the characters, writers often find themselves developing the plot. What follows are profiles that I constructed for the two main characters in *Priscilla Engaging in the Game of Politics*:

Ohio State Senator Daniel P. Callahan

Senator Callahan is a slender, dark-complexioned African American man, forty-nine years old and of medium height. His hair is close-shaven and receding from his forehead.

He wears old-fashioned wire-rimmed eyeglasses and a ring on his pinkie finger, but he does not care that a stone is missing. He is called "Mr. Polyester" behind his back because he wears polyester suits. He wears leather boots with elevated heels; people can hear him walking up and down the marble floors of the Ohio Senate.

He has an excellent command of English and an eloquent speaking voice, reminiscent of the great orators of the nineteenth century. When speaking on the Senate floor, he pivots from one side to the other as he addresses visitors in the gallery. He has perfect posture, always stands erect, and rarely slumps his shoulders. He walks fast, almost always as if he is in a hurry.

He is a proud and somewhat pompous man, an attitude he adopted to cope with others in the conservative, white, male-dominated Ohio Senate. A seasoned politician, Senator Callahan honed his political skills in the NAACP. He fights vigilantly for the rights of the underprivileged and Black people.

He has seniority in the Ohio Senate and enjoys the privileges of his office, such as prime office space and staff. He is a man of character; he hardly ever exhibits immoral behavior, yet he is the type of person who is always in your face. He is hardworking and unyielding about facilitating the needs of his constituents. The senator possesses a remarkable ability to maneuver the legislative process, getting bills passed, even while serving in the minority political party. An accountant by profession, the senator uses his financial expertise to wheel and deal with almost every legislative measure he supports or opposes. Senator Callahan is an esteemed politician.

The senator is very demanding of his staff; Priscilla is no exception. Although he appreciates Priscilla's talents, especially her loyalty to him, he takes advantage of her much too often.

The senator is married with children, and he and his family reside in his legislative district in Cincinnati. But he spends most of his private time at his apartment in the capital city of Columbus.

Priscilla J. "PJ" Austin

Priscilla is twenty-seven years of age, five feet, and four-and-a-half inches in height, but she often claims to stand five feet and five inches tall. African American, she is fair in complexion and has a small frame. Her hairstyle resembles that of the rock group, the Beatles. Her elegance is understated, but she dresses in masculine clothing: black, navy blue, and gray suits, with little color and gloss in her accessories, and she wears stylish high heels. In the late 1970s and early 1980s, some up–and–coming professional women imitated their male counterparts.

Priscilla carries a navy-blue leather attaché case, almost always with a recording device, a legal pad, a pen, and a calculator. She is bright, carefree, and enterprising, and she comes ready for her job in the Ohio Senate.

Priscilla is closely bound to her father—an itinerant Methodist minister—who has raised her to think like a man. But her father has done more: he has groomed her to participate in a life he could never have, to go after her heart's desire. She does as she pleases because she knows her father will rescue her if she gets into trouble, an attitude she transfers to the senator.

She plays the piano and sews.

She grew up in Prendergast in the Snowbelt of western New York, loves the cold and the snow, and is comfortable around people of all ethnicities; she attended the church-sponsored Livingstone College in North Carolina and The Ohio State University. After teaching political science at Florida A&M University for a mere two years, she accepts a post as a legislative aide with the Ohio state senator at the behest of her father to "relocate closer to home." (Columbus is within a five-hour drive to Prendergast, New York.)

A product of the 1960s Civil Rights Movement, she is proud of her heritage. A staunch feminist, her race, ethnicity, and gender are others' problems. Of mixed race and ethnicity, she is West African, British, and Choctaw on her paternal side, West African, Irish, and Cherokee on her maternal side—all of which she claims wholeheartedly.

Unassuming, Priscilla has agency and no problem exerting it. She resents the image of the demure female type. She is an aide in the Ohio Senate for a reason, not to become friends with any other staff. Her minister-father has taught her to keep her personal life to herself, so she is aloof and could not give a darn what anyone thinks of her. Moreover, she behaves as if her boss, Senator Callahan, is the only senator for whom she works. She often defies her boss, which puts her in the doghouse, as it were. But Priscilla does not appreciate the overbearing attitude of the senator. And when she has had enough of her boss, or anyone else, for that matter, she grows silent and keeps to herself. She never uses personal excuses and hardly ever apologizes, traits she learned from somewhere about successful men. She is picayune and rarely considers the consequences of her actions.

Priscilla is not above doing whatever she feels like doing to get whatever she wants, including having an affair with her boss, whom she merely tolerates.

But Priscilla never entirely comes to terms with the fact that politicians of the same political party form caucuses and that their staff collaborates on the caucus's agenda. Priscilla's primary role is to please her boss in her way of thinking, so that is how she proceeds.

Mostly though, Priscilla has a penchant for getting into a spot of trouble, and she so enjoys the sheer rush of a storm or two.

Figure 5. A view of the Ohio Statehouse from the South side

Naming Main Characters, Protagonists, and Supporting Characters

Authors must be attentive in naming the characters in their work. As a rule, I research names for characters based on their cultures and ethnic groups. For example, in *Special Envoy: Priscilla Journeys into Arab Islamic Territory*, I created an essential character, Abdul-Hakim Murshid Mus'ab. Abdul-Hakim means servant of the wise. In the story, he is the Minister of Cultural Affairs for Dubai and the nephew of the emir-prime minister of Dubai. His full name reflects his ethnicity, political role, and ties to a royal family. In another of my novels, *Three Metal Pellets*, I named the presidential hopeful Fleetwood Marshall Hollingsworth. Historically, many African Americans adopted the names and titles of prominent people for their children, especially the boys, such as Thomas Jefferson so-in-so or Major so-in-so, or William Edward Burghardt DuBois. Some even created impressive names, such as Fleetwood Marshall so-in-so.

In "the Priscilla Series," Priscilla's best friend, Julia Cahill, is based on a real-life acquaintance of the author, an African American Jew.

The Name Priscilla

The Reverend John Wesley Simms named me after Princess Margaret—Queen Elizabeth II's younger sister. I like that my name was borrowed from such a remarkable personality. But I did not think anyone would be interested in a story about a young woman named Margaret. My given name also reminds me of the cartoon character in *Dennis the Menace*.

So, why did I choose the name, Priscilla? Growing up in Jamestown, New York, I was a member of a threesome, a clique or coterie: Margaret, Lavon, and Priscilla. As for Lavon, the name did not fit the character. I chose, instead, the name of the third member of the group, Priscilla (Hodnett) Sanders. (I have her permission to acknowledge this fact.)

As it turned out, the name Priscilla has become an excellent fit for the fictitious character which brings us to a discussion about portraying contemporary professional African American (Black) women with agency in novels.

A Word about the Paucity of Novels about Contemporary Professional Black Women Protagonists with Agency: Possibilities for Black Women Authors and Other Writers of Fiction

Here, I explain why, earlier, I wrote: "The traditional publishing houses are not known for books whose main characters are contemporary professional African American women...." Although I intimated that this is the type of character I depict in my own writing, I did not mention that this characterization is sorely lacking in the literary canon.

Back in the late 1990s, when I penned my first novel, *Priscilla Engaging in the Game of Politics* (2016)—and which I initially copyrighted in 2004 and sometime earlier as *Playing the Game*—my editor at the time, informed me that he felt that readers might feel somewhat misled to find out, some three or more chapters into the book, that Priscilla is African American. He wrote that, up to that point in the story, readers were being led to believe the novel was about an upper-middle-class professional young woman growing up in New England. His comments troubled me, particularly the not-so-subtle implication there are no upper-middle-class African Americans in New England. Nevertheless, the editor put his true thoughts into words, which forewarned the rejection letters I eventually received from literary agents. Since I did not study creative writing in college and was unfamiliar with the racial undercurrents in the publishing industry, how was I to know that traditional publishers want(ed) "main characters who are Black" to be identified at the novel's beginning? Ridiculous. For sure, I did not know that editors and publishers regard(ed) novels about contemporary professional Black women— especially self-empowered Black women—as "incredible" and "unprofitable." Even though the subject matter reflected what the literary agents were looking for, after it occurred to them that my protagonist was, in fact, African American, they wrote to me that my manuscript was "not a good fit for us at this time," "lacks credibility," among other put-downs; and this was after the publication of Terry McMillan's *Waiting to Exhale* (1992) and Adichie's AMERICANAH (2013). So, now you know why I publish my work myself. What follows is an explanation of how such thinking has contributed to the scarcity of novels about contemporary professional Black women protagonists with agency.

Ironically, those early literary agents, and my first editor, too, were behind the eight ball—and perhaps, they still are. Circumstances in American society, as well as elsewhere, point to the need—the urgency is more like it—for literature about all of us more reflective of the times, which, by all indications, project African Americans and people of Hispanic origin as the majority population in the United States by the middle of the 21st century. Never mind that people of color will soon become the majority population around the globe, if not already. So the literature, especially novels, must reflect the changing demographics, of which African, African American, and other women of color are integral. Black professional women are everywhere: heads of state, members of the U.S. Congress and Parliaments, mayors, financial advisers, realtors, actresses, travel agents, law enforcement/military officers, play/script/screenwriters, special agents in the FBI, the CIA, and the NSA, golf/tennis pros, entrepreneurs/CEOs, professors/college presidents, the gamut. All authors might portray these kinds of characters, whether as the protagonists or in a supporting role, filling the void in the American literary canon and elsewhere, not to mention merely being relevant. Mostly though, we need to be proactive and build a body of literature for future generations to learn about African and African American peoples' more realistic and inspirational lives. Enough already with the multi-generational impoverished and uneducated single moms, the maids, the prostitutes, the prisoners, the narcotics addicts, the mean women, the former slaves, and the women "hungry for a man."

To demonstrate where the literature stands, we begin with Professor Carmen Rose Marshall's assessment of "why so few novels represent the Black professional woman (BPW) with agency in both her professional and private life." Marshall also examined the levels of agency that the protagonists evidence in the narratives *The Salt Eaters* and *Waiting to Exhale* and the readers' level of satisfaction with the novels they had read (Marshall 2004, 158).[3]

After identifying themselves by age, career choice, and the number of hours per week they read, the representative sample of 175 Black [American] professional women readers were then asked to identify the "realistic" novels they had read with the protagonist as a BPW with agency. Familiar names such as Toni Morrison, Terry McMillan, Alice Walker, Maya Angelou, Julie Dash, Bebe Moore Campbell, and Paule Marshall were listed the most and in that order. Books listed were the following: *Tar Baby*, *Waiting to Exhale*, *How Stella Got Her Groove Back*, *The Color Purple*, and *Daughters of the Dust* (161-162).

One might ask, "What is agency?" The term refers to the extent to which a protagonist possesses and exercises relative power, whether in battle, captivity, corporate settings, domestic and social environs, or whatever the situation. For

---

[3] References to the material on pages 151-162, 165-166, and 170 in *Black Professional Women in Recent American Fiction* are by permission of the publisher.

example, in a corporate setting, to what degree does the main character participate in management- or executive-level decision-making, such as strategic planning, establishing and managing budgets, recruitment, downsizing, and so on? More plainly put, to what extent does the protagonist demonstrate discernment, efficacy, and volition?

That 76 percent of the respondents in Marshall's survey were not satisfied with the novels that they had read (162) is telling. Most preferred that the protagonists or the main characters possess "professional traits," which they found missing in the books they had read (165-166). Toni Cade Bambara's *The Salt Eaters* and Terry McMillan's *Waiting to Exhale* were no exceptions. Rarely are the main characters even portrayed as self-empowered professionals in their workplaces. Hence, readers have no idea how these women perform their jobs, the job-related circumstances in which they work, and the like.

I believe one's writing mirrors one's worldview, generally influenced by upbringing, education, and life experiences. I was fortunate to have parents who knew who they were and taught my siblings and me accordingly. My father unabashedly used his community affiliations, such as the Rotary International in Jamestown, New York, to advance his agenda. The year was 1977, and he landed me the first professional post for a Black person with the local branch of Marlin-Rockwell TRW. I worked in the Computer Information Systems division, a job for which I was wholly ill-suited. Yet, my new peers were warm and inviting and helpful with my work. They even invited me to their homes, golfing, skiing, whatever. I knew of only one other Black professional in the company, and she worked in an office upstairs. Admittedly, at the time, I was unaware of the onslaught of Affirmative Action, and that the company's reputation was on the line. After coming to terms with the situation, I left and signed on as an assistant professor of political science at Florida A&M University, an HBCU in Tallahassee, for which my credentials were most suited.

I then served as a legislative aide in the Ohio Senate from 1980 to 1983 where I was the second Black person to serve in that capacity, and the first Black female, none of which mattered to me. Although we were a politically competitive lot, overall, my colleagues were cordial and amenable to helping me perform my job, even some of the staff from "the other side of the aisle." Meanwhile, personally, and professionally, I associated with more Black professionals than I ever knew existed, especially in the arts, business, politics, science, and technology. Perhaps that was due primarily to the location: I worked at the state capitol in the vicinity of The

Ohio State University, the likes of Battelle Memorial Institute, and a thriving Black middle-class.

We authors write primarily about what we know, and I am familiar with many Black professional women, none of whom are looking to men for fulfillment. Nor are they preoccupied with fulfilling some unachievable agenda for "the race." Therefore, in "the Priscilla Series," I write about a contemporary professional young woman who happens to be African American who pushes past what she deems as others' foolishness regarding her race, gender, and class. Nor does she require academic discourse or a publishing guru to affirm her; she exudes self-empowerment in the workplace and private life. Priscilla has agency—lots of it.

Another surprise in Marshall's findings was who the readers held accountable for the scarcity of such novels. Admittedly, I hold the publishers responsible, and 38 percent of Marshall's survey respondents agree. However, 34 percent of the respondents blame the writers for the shortage of such books (170)—which I contend is a clear call for more novels about BPW with agency.

Overlooked in Marshall's study was the responsibility of academicians. To the point, Juliana Makuchi Nfah-Abbenyi (1997, 2)[4], among others, speaks to the significance of being published and read and taught in academia and being acknowledged by one's counterparts, namely white feminists. Literature by Black women authors must first be accepted by their peers and incorporated into academia's curricula. Small wonder the participants in Marshall's survey seemingly overlooked books by Black women authors they had read in school and college. Could it be that they had not read any literature by Black women authors in school and college?

Two other factors need addressing. Elinettie Chabwera (2010, 1)[5] reminds us of geographical constraints at play when dealing with literature by Black women writers—generally confined to works primarily by African American women writers—which brings us to the other factor. Works performed by Black women writers from outside America are often "marginalized," relegated to categories of less significance (Boyce Davies 1994, 33).[6] The term "other" comes to mind.

Interestingly, Marshall published her work in the same year that *African Literature Today* devoted its 24th edition to New Women's Writing in AFRICAN

---

[4] By permission of Indiana University Press.
[5] Reprinted by permission of the author, Elinettie K. Chabwera, Ph.D.
[6] By permission of Taylor and Francis Group, LLC, a division of Informa plc.

LITERATURE (2004).[7] Ahead of the curve, African women writers have been crafting novels about female protagonists with agency since the late 1960s. Many African nations had not even attained independence from European rule. Yet, African women writers found ways to record and publish their stories. Consider, for example, Bessie Head's, *When Rain Clouds Gather* (1968), *Maru* (1971), and *A Question of Power* (1973), and Tsitsi Dangarembga's *Nervous Conditions* (1988). Then there is Professor Marie Umeh's biography of *Flora Nwapa, A Pen and a Press* which records the life and literary works of Nigeria's first female novelist and Africa's first female publisher—highly regarded as Chinua Achebe's literary sister and professional colleague (Umeh, 2010, xi, xxvi). As it so happened, Nwapa underwent a remarkable transition from her early works, such as *Efuru* (1966), to her highly acclaimed transformative work in her senescent years, most notably, her plays: *The First Lady* (1993) and *Conversations* (1993).

Other *African* women authors who write about protagonists with agency include but are not limited to the following: Nawal El Saadawi's *Woman at Point Zero* (1975)—lest we overlook the incredible life story of the author herself—Ama Ata Aidoo's *Changes: A Love Story* (1993), Virginia Phiri's *Highway Queen* (2010), and Marie NDiaye's *Three Strong Women* (2015). Like any well-crafted narrative, the themes of these ground-breaking works are universal. For example, Aidoo (1993) depicts, in intricate detail, the discord between contemporary professional men and women in Ghanaian society. This situation is particularly notable given women's advancement in the workplace, whereas, as Aidoo points out, in contrast, the roles of Ghanaian men, and men elsewhere, remain relatively unchanged. In yet another body of work, "Market Women" portrays the powerful West African women, mainly in Ghana, a.k.a., "GA Traditional Women."

If the main point is still unclear, consider Margot Lee Shetterly's *Hidden Figures: The Story of African-American Women Who Helped Win the Space War* (2016). Although a nonfiction work, authors can surely take a page from *Hidden Figures* and create plots about contemporary BPW with agency. The book's success and the movie version are a testament to the need for such material.

Marshall's *Black Professional Women in Recent American Fiction* is ultimately an undeniable assessment of the lack of novels about self-empowered contemporary professional Black [American] women protagonists in the workplace and their personal lives. Her findings offer possibilities for Black women authors, plus, I

---

[7] Ernest N. Emenyonu, Editor, *New Women's Writing in* AFRICAN LITERATURE, African Literature Today, Vol. 24, (Oxford: James Currey and Africa World Press, 2004).

contend, other fiction writers. Her findings also call for a follow-up assessment based on a larger, more representative sample of professional Black women readers on a broader scale.

Do not conclude this presentation as an attempt to interfere with your freedom of expression. Certainly not. Write about whatever you wish. But, if the void in the literature is to be filled, then by whom other than Black women writers. Moreover, if the traditional publishing industry rejects your work, publish it yourself. I do.

This is an excellent place to mention that, around 2013, I interviewed three editors, one of whom, unbeknown to me at the time, was in the United Kingdom. After reading *Priscilla Engaging in the Game of Politics*, the British editor informed me of the potential for narratives like mine, as she pointed out the lack of literature about contemporary professional Black women in the literary canon. Little did I realize the depth of her words back then.

The Protagonist Is Key.

Create a main character or protagonist with whom your readers can relate.
Priscilla is the protagonist in the entire Priscilla Series. In the first novel, *Priscilla Engaging in the Game of Politics,* after teaching as a political science professor at Florida A&M University for only two years, her father mysteriously asks her to relocate to a place closer to home. So her father's request interests readers because it was he who had encouraged her to take the job in the first place. Indeed, something like this has happened to you or someone you know.

One way to show her father's request, and Priscilla's response, is to use dialogue between the two of them.
In so doing, enhance your readers' ability to envision the father and the daughter talking. For example, describe their facial expressions, their body language, and any of their movement, maybe even as they reminisce about related incidents. In my own fiction, I use a lot of reflection in the form of flashbacks.

Show what happens along the protagonist's journey.
I created scenes depicting Priscilla finding a way to honor her father's request and her eventual relocation to Columbus, Ohio, near their home in Prendergast, New York. Like Peyton Place, Prendergast is fictitious. Most people who know me know the setting is, in fact, Jamestown, New York. But Jamestown is such a common name that I chose to name the city after its founder, James Prendergast. The point, however, is to show the protagonist's journey.

Select the narrator's point of view.
From Priscilla's perspective, readers learn what her life was like while growing up in Prendergast and all else that she experiences along her journey.

Show the Protagonist Developing. Coming-of-age stories convey character development, one way or another.
By the end of each book in the Priscilla Series, for example, Priscilla has evolved from the time when she first set out, as follows:
- From a self-centered, sheltered "daddy's girl" to a sophisticated woman.
- From innocence and self-absorption to awareness and sensitivity.
- From attachment to her father and traditional family life to a member of a nontraditional and extended family.

53

- ○ From a political science professor to a legislative aide to a PR consultant-turned-intelligence agent.
- ○ Ultimately, she adopts an expanded worldview.

> Throughout the movie version of John Grisham's *Pelican Brief*, Darby Shaw, played by Julia Roberts, develops from a law student enamored with her professor to a strong and independent woman.

Now that you have some idea about the main character and the other characters in your story, let us develop plot(s).

If you have not already written a short story or begun a novel, consider using the exercise you just started about the three people searching for a hotel suite in the year 2050. But before you can construct a plot, you need to know English composition and quite a bit more about creative writing.

Recall my notes in the Preface about English composition. If you have already taken an English composition course and especially a creative writing course, none of this is new to you. Still, you might need to hone your skillset before starting your first significant manuscript. So keep that grammar book and those writing-standards books handy, lest we forget the *MLA* and the *CMS*, which can save you considerable time and much money during the editing phase.

> If you are unfamiliar with these basic creative writing standards, consider enrolling in a creative writing class. Most colleges offer these courses at the introductory levels. Besides honing your creative writing skills, you will also learn the latest computer software.

Create Plot(s).

In the section of *The Young Writer at Work* entitled "The Importance of Plot," Rehder (1977) quotes, at length, from *A Handbook to Literature* by William Flint Thrall and Addison Hibbard:

> ... [I]t is perhaps more helpful to describe plot than to define it with generalities. The incidents which are part of a plot are, it has been said, (1) *planned*; they are preconceived by the author; they spring from his conscious thought; they are not simply taken over from life. No matter how realistic an author may be, he must arrange and select his incidents according to a plot purpose since life itself only rarely, if ever, unfolds according to the plans of a fiction plot. Plot is, too, (2) *a series of actions* moving from a beginning through a logically related sequence to a logical and natural outcome. One incident—an afternoon's cruise—does not make a plot, no matter how interesting the afternoon may have been. Several incidents—if the story is one of action—are essential. There must at least be a beginning, a middle, and an end in the interplay of the opposing forces and, most frequently, this means three or more episodes. And these incidents grow one upon another; incident two following by a causal relationship from incident one, and incident three following, by this same relationship, from two. The difference between a simple narrative and a story of plot is the difference between a calendar and a knitted scarf. In the calendar the pages follow one another logically, but in the scarf the texture is the result of weaving one thread over and under another. In a story with closely knit plot the removal of one incident would bring the whole structure down upon one's head much as though he had removed an important prop from the scaffolding for a building. In a story of mere unrelated incidents, the removal of one incident would leave, simply, a gap. (3) This interrelationship of action is the result, as has been said, of *the interplay of one force upon another*.... Plot is, in this sense, an artificial rather than a natural ordering of events. Its function is to simplify life by imposing order upon it. It would be possible, though most tedious, to recite *all* incidents, *all*

events, *all* thoughts which pass through the minds of one or more characters during a period of, say, a week. And somewhere in this recital might be a buried story. But the demands of plot stipulate that the author *select* from this welter of event and reflection those items which have a certain unity, which point to a certain end, which have a common interrelationship, which represent not more than two or three threads of interest and activity (171).

Hopefully, the aforementioned sheds some light on the importance of creating plot(s). I especially appreciate Thrall's and Hibbard's comparison between "a simple narrative" (the "calendar") and "a story of plot" (the "knitted scarf"). Perhaps you can think of other authors who have written more complex plots. Although ours is not a dichotomous world, the authors' main point still holds.

Create a Storyboard. (Some authors draft outlines.) Like a road map, a storyboard, or a design, keeps you on track.

Other authors jot down notes on index cards or sheets of paper and post them on the wall of the room where they write. Then, as the story develops, they rearrange the index cards and the paper sheets on the wall accordingly. Sometimes they insert new scenes and remove others that no longer fit. Of course, you can also use Sticky Notes, OneNote, or some other method to record your story.

I am a pen-and-paper writer. I write, in longhand, on legal pads; then I type from my notes on my laptop, which brings me more ideas, strengthening the storyline. I hardly ever use an outline or a storyboard. Believe it or not, I have no idea where the story is going most of the time. I just keep moving my pen across the page as the words flow from my head. But not everyone can write this way, so do consider developing outlines and using storyboards.

> Although many people have spoken these words before, I prefer country-and-western singer Hank Williams, who once said, "God gives me the words; I just write them down."

Create Conflict for the Main Character (the Protagonist).

In the discussion in Rule #3, you began drafting a story about three people seeking a hotel suite in the year 2050. If you have yet to draft another story, continue building on that writing exercise to maneuver this next part.

Perhaps there is something that the protagonists need or want, but something or someone is blocking their way.

You might create scenes challenging the characters' wits.

Or maybe one of them does something that challenges her value system. For example, she steals a passport or a credit card to reserve the hotel suite. But the main characters (protagonists) stepping out of a taxi, walking into a hotel, and handing the receptionist their credit cards do not make for a compelling plot.

Here, we examine a scene from one of my novels that demonstrates the significance of creating plot, with conflict accompanied by suspense—taken from *Mystery in Harare: Priscilla's Journey into Southern Africa* (2017). The following passage portrays the claustrophobic Priscilla on the run from an assassin inside the Rustenburg Platinum Mine in South Africa:

> Priscilla looked up in a panic as the siren shrieked and the loud-speaker shouted words that she could not quite make out. But she knew the sound of panic when she heard it.
>
> She knew she could not outrun the man who she sensed was already following her. Nor could she breathe with any ease too far down in this immense cavern. She already had walked past a few soldiers without any problem, but the sound of the siren had put them on full alert. Had they mistakenly allowed her to pass? She knew she would be stopped by the next group of soldiers.
>
> Priscilla used her lighted helmet to search the mine's walls for any cavity she thought she could reach. Finally, she found one. She struggled but failed to climb the steep wall. But when it seemed as if she would have to continue walking along the path, she heard the sound of rapidly approaching footsteps.

All right now, she reasoned, *before I completely lose my mind, think.*

Her eyes caught sight of a pile of tools on one of the huge carts on the tracks. Most of the tools were unfamiliar to her, and some looked too big to carry. So she picked up a couple of familiar tools, a small hammer, and a stake and put them in her back pants pockets. *Never know when these'll come in handy,* she said to herself. *Might have to dig myself out of here.* She felt better with a weapon in her hand. This time, Priscilla was in self-defense mode. So when she mused about digging herself out of there, she was really thinking about doing battle with the man whom she thought was a South African Army captain. She already suspected that the vicious villain probably would get the better of her. But she was also acutely aware of her own trademark: none of the people she fought ever came back for seconds. Her hands trembled as she patted the hammer and stake in her back pants pocket. Then she remembered the time she took a butcher's knife to a street fight back during her high school years in Prendergast. She breathed faster with each thought and each step.

Frightened nearly out of her wits, Priscilla kept talking to herself to muster her courage. Then she remembered someone shouting at them during their tour to "lean up against the wall." She hobbled sideways against the wall until at long last she reached the lift. She was sweating profusely. She felt her heart beating fast, too. She steadied herself near the lift, leaning as hard as she could against the wall because she feared the footsteps, she had been hearing were those of someone looking to do her harm, and she did not want him to hear her moving.

But soon she saw that those footsteps she had been hearing belonged to the miners—either walking towards the lift or getting off it and heading out the mine. Priscilla was caught between the miners' changing shifts.

Since she was clearly visible near the lift, some of the miners stopped and stared.

Suddenly she whispered, "Help me, please. Help me. Hide me." Then she pointed to a place high up the steep mine wall.

There are certain words, expressions, and symbols that are universal, and the image of someone in distress is one such expression. And one never knows when the kindness of strangers will come to the rescue. The simple compassionate interest that Priscilla had shown in the miners during her earlier tour of the mine was just about to pay off.

By the expressions on their faces, it seemed that several of the men recognized Priscilla from her earlier trip inside the mine that day. Obviously, too, they were making an effort to understand what this mysterious little soldier, who was noticeably panting, was saying. It did not take them long to determine both that "he" was in distress and what "he" was asking of them.

A few of them nodded and then escorted the little soldier a short distance away from the lift before hoisting "him" up.

The little soldier—Priscilla—was now able to feel some cracks and crevices in the wall. "He" hung on tight and lifted "himself" even higher.

As the little soldier was settling "himself" in "his" hideout, a large crevice, a few of the other miners wisely decided to create a diversion. They noisily began to load one of the huge carts with dirt.

Their timing was perfect because Priscilla's stalker was not far away (Simms-Maddox 2017, 396-398).

Now, read what Rehder (1977) says about suspense creating conflict in a plot:

The desire to witness action has always been inherent in those who want to hear a story. Their command to the writer is not, 'Tell me how you felt. Tell me what you thought.' Rather, it is 'Tell me what they did and why. Keep me in suspense.' For in a story, if not in life, *we want conflict* [Emphasis mine], we want to be led on through the moments of suspense like a donkey following a carrot dangled before him. And most of us prefer to know that something is going to happen and to be kept wondering when and why rather than to be hit by a surprise.

Surprise comes when an unexpected event is flung at the reader without preparation. The suspense comes when we tease, give hints, and at the same time without information from the reader. Suspense is an emotional reaction generated by the reader's ignorance of whether a character will get what she wants or goes down in defeat. At the end of the story, although the character's fate may come as a surprise, it should have been so well prepared for by the writer that in retrospect the final action seems inevitable. At the end of a story we are done with suspense—we want the satisfaction of catching up with the carrot.

But suspense and surprise do not make a plot…

In other words, plot, as it was defined by the Greeks, has a design that arises from the internal structure of the play. …But Greek tragedy, at its best, gives importance to both the mechanics and to the character in conflict, meshing them as partners (169-170).

I agree that "suspense and surprise do not make a plot." There is also persuasiveness, intrigue, and other features. These are not mere differences in semantics. Does the protagonist do something wholly unexpected? Does something entirely unforeseen happen to her? Whatever the action, is the narrative persuasive? Does it depict enough intrigue to keep readers turning the pages?

Although the central tenets for creative writing advanced by Rehder and others before her still hold, today, many authors might find the analogy of readers behaving like donkeys trying to catch up with a carrot somewhat off-putting.

Indubitably, *writing styles* have advanced in ways unimaginable in previous decades, but acclaimed contemporary authors still adhere to the central tenets of writing, especially in their novels. For example, accomplished authors from the late twentieth to the early twenty-first centuries—Michael Ondaatje and Stieg Larsson come to mind—demonstrate significantly different writing styles than, say, accomplished authors from the early to mid-twentieth century, such as F. Scott Fitzgerald, Ernest Hemingway, Rex Stout, and Richard Wright, not to mention some of their predecessors, such as Jane Austen, T. S. Eliot, Alfred Lloyd Tennyson,

Edgar Allan Poe, Agatha Christie, and Sir Arthur Conan Doyle. Put another way, do not confuse writing styles with the *standards* for writing fiction.

Rehder further asserts, "Any story that employs plot as action and necessity has an ending in which the [heroine] succeeds or fails, or finds a solution of sorts to recompense [her] for apparent failure. We are defining plot as an organic one in which the incidents seem not to be artificially introduced. The results of the conflict then rise naturally from the preceding action and the story is able to flow rather than march forward, whatever its level of action may be" (175). Such is the case with all the previously cited authors.

Try not to let the creation of conflict baffle you. Think about whatever frightens you. I call upon my phobias, such as those that cause imbalance, like acrophobia and vertigo. I also borrow from early silent and black-and-white movies, especially film noir. Apart from their use of light and simple props, such as one room, a moving train, or a rolling screen as a backdrop, the early film directors were adept at creating cadence or rhythm, what Rehder calls "flow." Like the first movie directors, modern-day authors must depict rhythmic movement towards or against someone, something, or someplace in their stories. But it is the unexpected that breaks the flow and grips readers. Essentially, conflict brings reality to the fore. For example, the previous passage from *Mystery in Harare: Priscilla's Journey into Southern Africa* is one of several scenes portraying Priscilla in that platinum mine. Each one creates layer upon layer of intrigue and suspense toward the climax. In the end, no one, not even Priscilla, can fathom what she has done to survive. Yet, something about her background and personality suggests that no matter her circumstance, she will prevail—ergo, the realistic ending, what Rehder calls a "real resolution," which brings us to the final part of this discussion.

Near the end of the section of *The Young Writer at Work* in "The Importance of Plot," Rehder identifies four stages or critical incidents distinguishable in a workable plot: an opening situation, a complication of sorts, the pivotal scene or climax, and a fundamental resolution or a decisive ending. In the end, she notes, "Many 'plot writers' are able to keep a story going by presenting a trap and then making us want to know how the main character is going to get out of the trap" (175). Can you apply any of these elements to your writing? Their construction is paramount because "the primary function of plot is to translate character into action" (197).

Put Your Protagonist in the Corridors of Political Power (or Whatever the Principal Setting Is).

Since many plots in my novels involve politics, I tend to put Priscilla in the corridors of political power. For *Priscilla Engaging in the Game of Politics*, the Ohio Senate is the principal setting. For example, after I show Priscilla relocating to Ohio, I portray her working in the Ohio Senate as a legislative aide, which is how she gets closer to home. In so doing, I created scenes showing her inside her new office, interacting with her colleagues, observing historical artifacts, riding the elevators, walking up and down the imposing marble staircases, and the like. I also constructed scenes showing her relationships with other staff, the senators, and the lobbyists and describing the committee activity and the senators voting.

For Michael Ondaatje's Count Laszlo de Almásy in *The English Patient*, the principal setting is the Gilf El-Kebir, a desert plateau in Egypt. For Stieg Larsson's Lisbeth Salander in *The Girl Who Played with Fire*, pick a scene; her father's farmhouse in Gosseberga, Sweden, is etched in my mind. And so it is with Tolkien's Frodo and his entourage at The Bridge of Khazad-Dûm in *The Fellowship of the Ring*. For someone such as myself, who is pretty much self-taught, I eventually learned how to create these types of scenes; so, too, must you.

The Title of Your Book and Its Chapter Headings Often Occur to You after You've Completed Your Manuscript.

By now, you are aware that the original title for *Priscilla Engaging in the Game of Politics* was *Playing the Game*, but *Playing the Game* was overly used. The new title is more reflective of the storyline.

That was not the only time that I changed a copyrighted book title. The title of my third novel, *Three Metal Pellets*, was originally *El Qâhira Overlooks the River Nile*. *Three Metal Pellets* came from a critical chapter in the book. As it turned out, the new title also aided in creating a more distinctive book cover. Meanwhile, the first title then becomes an *alternative title*.

As for chapter headings, not all authors use chapter headings. If you prefer chapter headings, indicate what readers can expect in each chapter. I like chapter headings, but they are not a necessary element for novels. Below are three examples from *Priscilla Engaging in the Game of Politics*:

- o   In Chapter One, "Teaching, a Noble Profession," Priscilla sets out on her first full-time teaching job at Florida A&M University because she believes she is fulfilling the long-held passion of her beloved father. He first planted the expression in her mind. In honor of her father, Priscilla does her best to fulfill his expectations of her as a professor.

- o   In Chapter Fifteen, "The Scenic Route," Priscilla shows readers in intricate detail what life was like growing up in the Snowbelt of western New York.

- o   Chapter Thirty is entitled "A Defection in the Ranks" because, after the 1982 elections in Ohio, Senate Democrats win control of that chamber. But one among them defects and joins with the Senate Republican Caucus, thereby giving the Republicans control of the Ohio Senate again.

The previous discussions on creative writing standards covered in Rules #3 and #4 are far from comprehensive. I barely scratched the surface, which is why I encourage emerging authors to enroll in a creative writing course at the college level and to practice writing. If you cannot attend college at this time, ask your local librarian to get a copy of Jessie Rehder's *The Young Writer at Work* (1977) for you. Also, I highly recommend getting one or more of the other books on writing standards discussed earlier in this handbook. In this way, you can begin learning the criteria essential for creative writing on your own.

We turn now to the fifth and final rule in my writing creed.

Rule #5: *Never Give Up—Keep Right on Writing.*

Becoming a successful indie book author and publisher does not just happen. For most authors, success—however, measured—comes after many, many failures— still, the many, many failures fuel one's determination to write better and publish even more.

Apart from being an avid reader, producing work that reads naturally takes much life experience. For example, when trials and tribulations and unwelcomed experiences come into your life, write about them. A loved one gets shot and killed; write about it. You walked inside the enormous pyramid in the world; write about it. You learned a new hobby; write about it. Your significant other stole all your savings and investments; write about it. Someone called you out of your name; write about it. One day, these experiences and everything else that happens in your life will benefit your narratives; when people read the stories, they will believe the plots are actual.

Be steadfast because—just like anything else you do, such as exercising or dieting— it is not easy to resume once you stop.

It takes much time, continuous effort, and money to produce excellent quality material, attain an effective marketing strategy, and attain a cadre of followers who purchase and read your books. So, keep at it.

The next exercise concludes this section about developing a writing regimen and following the standards.

Prolific writers develop régimes suitable to their situation.

Instructions:
You might already have drafted an outline of your writing program at this point. As you progress in your writing career, always be mindful of what works best for you. Bear in mind that some writers develop different habits along the way. So, it is all right if how, when, and where you write today differs from how you write later. The point is to develop a régime that works best for your situation right now.

Rule #5: Never Give Up—Keep Right on Writing.

In the space provided below, write a description of your views about this particular rule. Then, continue building your writing regimen. (You might want to use a pencil so you can edit easily.)

_____
_____
_____
_____
_____
_____
_____
_____
_____
_____

Remember: if you are serious about establishing your writing career, developing a regimen is crucial. Consider starting in increments. Before you know anything else, you will have developed a regimen best suited to your situation.

Now, let us take the first step to become a serious author.

Look at all those books! One or more of them could be yours.

Figure 6. People in front of bookshelves by Ondrej Bocek, unsplash.com

Step One: Budget for Your Writing Career.

Conduct your writing career like a business. *Establish a budget.* Capital is necessary to purchase products and retain professional services, such as the following:

- ✓ A certified public accountant (CPA) for advice and help filing your income and corporate tax returns and sales taxes from book sales.
- ✓ Legal counsel for advice on incorporating and reading contracts. One of the reasons that some authors search endlessly for literary agents is because of their expertise in reading and interpreting publishing contracts. To some extent, having a literary agent—about which we discuss later—lessens the need for a contract or an intellectual property rights attorney. However, the necessity of retaining legal counsel adept at reading and interpreting publishing contracts and counseling you about your intellectual property rights cannot be overstated.
- ✓ Editing fees can range from $3,500 to over $5,000 per manuscript of 75,000-to-100,000 words or more.
- ✓ Professional membership dues and conference registration fees.
- ✓ Fees to exhibit at conferences and book fairs.
- ✓ Graphic artists/designers for artwork/design for book covers, business cards, posters, convention banners, a professional logo, domain names, and a web administrator for website design and maintenance, as well as a social media manager and a publicist.
- ✓ Photographers (not your friends and relatives, unless, of course, they are professionals).
- ✓ Publishing (See Step Four: "Getting Published-The Essentials").
- ✓ Associated costs include, but are not limited to, the following:
  - o Software, such as Adobe Acrobat Pro, Grammarly, Audible, Hindenburg, Microsoft Office Suite, even antivirus protection.
  - o Paper, ink cartridges, an all-purpose printer, and the like.
  - o Delivery services—for example, UPS and FedEx.
  - o Cellular phone, laptop computer, desktop computer, thumb disks, broadband internet access, Wi-Fi, wireless microphones, and amps for podcasts (optional).
  - o Postage, packaging, and shipping/handling.

- ○ Print-on-demand and offset printing.
- ○ Reference guides—for example, grammar books, dictionaries, and writing standards.
- ○ Travel, lodging, and meals.
- ○ Miscellaneous expenditures.

Hire a graphic artist/designer to create your logo. I use different parts of my logo for different purposes. For example, I mostly use the spilled ink bottle and quill—created by my brother, John Simms, an artist—on my copyright page. My name and title were added by my sister, Jina McGriff, a graphic artist/designer. She also designs my stationery, business cards, convention banners, flyers, website, et cetera. And I recently started using my boxed initials for the spine on my book covers. Although the choice is yours, keep the artwork professional. Then visit the U.S. Patent and Trademark Office at https://www.uspto.gov/ to register your trademark, that is, a ™, to protect your intellectual property.

You might also find it practical to hire a web administrator to design and maintain your website.

A Word about Establishing Your Writing Career as a Business

Although the intricacies about how to start a business and operate one are beyond the scope of this handbook, I do however recommend two sources I believe will help you along those lines.

Claudia Reuter's *Yes, You Can Do This! How Women Start Up, Scale Up, and Build The Life They Want* (2020) is an excellent resource. Reuter speaks primarily to women and women with children who have left the workplace and recommends that they take control of their lives by becoming entrepreneurs, thereby creating a life for themselves—something for emerging authors to consider. Toward the end of her book, Reuter provides a business checklist for aspiring entrepreneurs, and this handbook offers a checklist of publishing essentials exclusively for authors.

As for the second source, James P. Nettles' *Business Essentials for Writers: How to Make Money in an Ever-Changing Industry* (2019) speaks directly to writers in all facets of the publishing industry and focuses primarily on making your creative [writing] pursuit profitable (Nettles 2019, 12).[8] His book, like this handbook, expressly targets writers.

Nettles defines people's roles in the business, such as fans and customers, writers, agents, publicists, and web admins, and how they fit into its goals. He outlines ways to build a foundation with a realistic business plan. He provides crucial information about sales and marketing, such as defining your market, developing a marketing plan, sales channels, and more. And, like Reuter, Nettles expounds on setting up and managing operations, starting with the author herself at the helm as CEO. Ultimately, he covers the legalities, the tools of the trade, social media, website development, financing and accounting, and many other business essentials.

The author is incredibly adept at the ever-changing role of technology in the publishing industry and is exceptionally gifted in showing writers how to use technology to advance their business. I am confident that Nettles' book will come in handy for all authors, including the more advanced and indie publishers—a must-read for anyone entering the writing and publishing fields.

---

[8] By permission of the author, James P. Nettles.

What I most admire about Nettles is his proclamation: "Forget the starving artist. Be the *thriving* artist" (Nettles 2019, 19), a topic covered later in this handbook in "A Word about Pricing."

I first met Jim Nettles when he conducted a ZOOM session with the North Carolina Writers' Network (NCWN) https://www.ncwriters.org/ Metro-North Region, which encompasses Cabarrus and Rowan counties just north of Charlotte, NC. Jim demonstrated how to use MailerLite to create, distribute, and grow newsletter subscriptions with much patience and zeal. He taught us how to use our affiliates to expand our market reach in another session. I also learned about Claudia Reuter at a monthly meeting of the Metro-North Region. As I read her book, I became more impressed with her story, especially by sharing advice to women about becoming entrepreneurs.

For more information about the benefits of joining professional associations and conferences, see Step Six: "Promote and Sell Your Book."

For now, wrap your head around the fact that successful authors are, indeed, entrepreneurs.

We turn now to Step Two: "Equip yourself with the proper tools" to write.

Step Two: If You're Serious about Writing
and Getting Published,
Equip Yourself with the Proper Tools.

Although much of what is listed below can be found in the latest Microsoft Office Suite, authors need to familiarize themselves with various reference tools, such as these, and use them wisely. I refer to these tools as *confidence builders* because the more you use them, the more confident you become about your writing.

- ➤ Acquire the latest edition of the following:
  - ✓ A dictionary, such as *Merriam-Webster's Collegiate Dictionary*
  - ✓ An English grammar book
  - ✓ A thesaurus, such as *Roget's International Thesaurus*
  - ✓ *The Chicago Manual of Style*
  - ✓ *The MLA Handbook*
  - ✓ A world atlas
  - ✓ Religious texts include the Bible, the Quran, the Bhagavad-Gita, the Torah, and the Tengyur. (For example, one cannot apply Christian biblical text to cultures and practitioners of the Islamic faith or of any other faith, for that matter.)
- ➤ Obtain a journal, a batch of legal pads, index cards, post-its, thumb disks, as well as pens and pencils.
- ➤ Obtain a computer with Microsoft Word, Adobe Acrobat Pro DC, Grammarly, and broadband internet service.

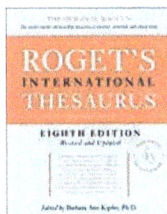

Step Three: Retain a Competent Editor.

Have you finished your novel? Has a trusted source—for example, a beta reader—reviewed your manuscript? Are you ready to turn the document over to an editor? Wherever you are in the writing process, it might be best to take a break from it all. Then, perform one more once-over, and send it to your editor. (See Appendix A for sample submission to an editor.)

If you do not yet have an editor, now is the time to locate one suitable for editing your work. Consider the following ways:
- ✓ Ask another author for referrals.
- ✓ Leaf through acknowledgments and forewords in books.
- ✓ Read book sections in newspapers and magazines or wherever you stay up to date on books.
- ✓ Travel in circles where professionals, such as authors, editors, literary agents, and publishers are likely easily accessible, including writers' conferences, book fairs, festivals, book signings, and trade shows.
- ✓ Contact faculty in the departments of English and literature at community colleges and universities.
- ✓ Watch BBC, C-Span, and PBS for author interviews and book-event coverage, such as the Miami Book Fair.
- ✓ Search for podcasts and blogs produced by noted authors.
- ✓ Inquire at public libraries and colleges and universities
- ✓ Search online for editors in the following organizations:
  - o National Association of Independent Writers & Editors
  - o Editorial Freelancers Association (EFA)*
  - o American Copy Editors Society
  - o North Carolina Writers' Network
  - o Authors' and writers' conferences and trade shows

*Early in the decade 2010, I accessed the EFA online and was surprised at the information about book editors. I landed three—darn good ones, too. Whichever organization you choose, you will be prompted to respond to a few questions, such as those listed below:

- o Keywords about your manuscript and writing style.
- o Genre, such as fiction, poetry, nonfiction, short stories, and subgenre, such as fantasy, sci-fi, romance, mystery, LGBTQ, YA/MG.... Mine are fiction: coming-of-age, mysteries, and thrillers.
- o According to your responses, a list of editors pops up.
  - Read about the kind of work the editors prefer.
  - Read their biographies and samples of their work. (Many are accomplished authors editing for a second income. Some even edit full-time.)
  - The editors' fee structures are also available, which are typically based on the word count, the number of pages in your manuscript, and the extent to which your work needs editing.
- o Be mindful of a clause regarding *nondisclosure*. The odds are none of these editors will "borrow" or "leak" your story. Nevertheless, protect your work. If no such clause exists, ask for one.

Editors' expertise varies from manuscript evaluation and developmental editing to copyediting to proofreading.

Some provide marketing services, and one might even function as your literary agent. To generate a proposed fee for their services, editors, of course, usually require *a sample of your writing*. So be prepared and patient in retaining an editor most suited to your writing style.

After your manuscript is professionally edited, you will then need a literary agent to sell it for you to a publisher, assuming, of course, you are trying to get picked up by a traditional publisher. Either way, "A Word about Literary Agents, Writing Query Letters, and Retaining a Contract Lawyer…" can help you along the way.

A Word about Literary Agents, Writing Query Letters, and Retaining a Contract Lawyer or an Intellectual Property Rights Attorney

At this stage of the process, it is not uncommon for aspiring authors to surmise, "I thought I was done when I got my manuscript edited. But now you're telling me that I've got to expend more time and effort searching for a literary agent, too!" Sorry. But when you finished your manuscript, you were only midway through the process. Now you must put on your enterprising and public relations caps and thrust yourself wholeheartedly into the publishing realm. Toward that end, if you want all your arduous work to pay off, either you will land a literary agent or sign on with a hybrid publisher or learn how to publish your work yourself.

For authors who are satisfied with their edited manuscript and excited about testing the waters to find out whether their work is, in fact, ready for publication, it is time to learn how to land *a literary agent*. Why is that? The simple answer is literary agents are professionals whose primary purpose is to sell an author's manuscript to a publisher, without whom authors have a tough row to hoe. More plainly put, literary agents do most of that work for the author, but we authors must also share in the hoeing, something that we will cover shortly.

For authors who prefer to sign on with a hybrid publisher, you also need to learn how to do some of what authors searching for a literary agent must learn and do, such as making a pitch and writing a query letter. Why is that? Like traditional publishers, hybrids also adhere to publishing standards and protocols.

Authors who want to learn how to publish their work themselves might find information in this discussion practical as well.

"Why else should I get a literary agent?" They are excellent facilitators of your work—if you can land one. Below is a shortlist of what they do best:
- o   Get your manuscript read quicker.
- o   Put your manuscript in front of an acquisition's editor.
- o   Read contracts to ensure as much as possible is in your favor.
- o   Negotiate subsidiary rights and obtain bonuses (escalators) for promotional events, such as television appearances.
- o   Negotiate and track payments to the author and much more.

Hopefully, I have your attention.

Now, lean forward as we address financial matters, something you need to know about before signing on with a literary agent.

Compensation

Reputable literary agents do not charge fees for anything until they sell your manuscript to a publisher, and then their fee (commission) is spelled out in their contract. Beware of agents who are *not* affiliated with professional associations because they tend to charge fees for the following services:

- o *Administrative or Office fees.* Many people of any profession are familiar with the phrase "costs associated with doing business" or "skin in the game." Where once authors might have been asked to pay for copying, postage, and long-distance telephone calls, today, electronic devices efficiently provide email, unlimited texts, long-distance telephone calls, and even docu-sign agreements. Professional literary agents rarely, if ever, charge for administrative or office fees.
- o Frowned upon and prohibited by professional associations and even regarded as unethical are *reading fees*, ranging from $25.00 - $500.00 or more. Think about it. Why pay a literary agent to read your manuscript when this is what she purports to do in the first place?
- o *Critiquing fees.* If your work is unpublishable, a professional literary agent will refer you to an editor or recommend that you have your work edited by someone else of your choosing. However, if you receive systematic evaluations of that nature, you might consider retaining a more experienced editor. It is one thing to have your manuscript rejected because it "is not a good fit for our purposes at this time." Still, it is an entirely different matter to receive several evaluations, noting, "Your manuscript is unpublishable."

My advice: avoid literary agents requesting fees for anything. Their job is first, and foremost, to sell your manuscript to a publisher. After that, you compensate them with the agreed-upon commission(s). If the agent insists on a fee or deposit upfront, discontinue the relationship. Full stop.

How then are agents compensated? Generally, literary agents receive a 15% commission on domestic sales and a 20% commission for foreign sales of an author's manuscript. There are, of course, exceptions to this rule, particularly with specific formats and other factors, such as the acquisition of subsidiary rights, for example, performance, television, film, permission rights, and English translation. Regardless, now you know upfront what to expect.

Landing a Literary Agent

"All right," you might say, "I'm interested. So, how exactly do I find a literary agent?" There are many ways of doing this. I recommend accessing the Association of Authors' Representatives website at https://www.aar-online.org, the National Writers Union at https://www.nwu.org, and similar types of organizations.

You need to know something about the person you are asking to represent you and your work. So, add the *Guide to Literary Agents* to your library collection. This reference book contains information about the agents' affiliations, backgrounds, experiences, and levels of success with manuscript sales.

Begin by searching the guide's index for your genre, i.e., fiction, poetry, nonfiction, YA/MG, and so forth, where the names of the literary agents representing your type of work are listed. If you write fiction, as I do, start there; notice the subgenres, too. These data will be advantageous to connect with the appropriate literary agent.

Inside the guide's back book cover is a list of icons that signify how the literary agencies are listed, for example, "agency not seeking new clients," "agency located outside the U.S. and Canada," or "agency seeking both new and established writers."

For example, this symbol indicates that an agency is not seeking new clients.

When you locate an agency seeking new clients, scroll down to the icon symbolizing a key; this is the agent's specialization. Look for "Actively seeking …." If your manuscript does not fit this description, proceed to the following agent on your list, and so on.

Notice that literary agents also list the number of clients they have, the genres they represent, the percentage of emerging authors and the percentage of unpublished authors they are willing to accept, their guidelines for submitting query letters, and other information.

Read the section on conferences. Take your time in selecting the ones most suitable, convenient, and affordable to your situation. You might find yourself choosing to register for one or more conferences where you can easily interact with other authors like yourself, not to mention chance upon an opportunity to make an "elevator pitch" about your story to a literary agent. (This subject is discussed in Appendix F, "The Making of the Priscilla Series.") You might, however, experience a little difficulty deciding which workshops, seminars, roundtable and panel discussions, and other sessions to attend, all of which are conducted by authors, editors, literary agents, service providers, technology gurus, publishers, and the like, and, run concurrently, at that. You can even schedule an appointment to pitch your manuscript to a literary agent. Literary agents often attend these conferences with an eye for new authors. There is almost always an exhibition arena, occupied by booksellers and buyers, technology-service providers, and even book reviewers, such as Apple, Audible, Amazon, Bowker, Google Play Books, Hindenburg, Ingram, Kobo, PublishDrive, and *Publishers Weekly*. Authors with impressive booths sell and sign their books. Let us not overlook the celebrated authors serving as keynote speakers and conducting master classes on one topic or another.

Writing Query Letters

Most literary agents prefer one-page submissions; they do not have all day to read your query letter. (The *Guide to Literary Agents* shows writers how to craft a query letter and provides samples.) Agents receive hundreds and thousands of query letters, so yours must be concise and impressive. If, for example, your manuscript is fiction, omit photos, artwork, and graphics. Serious writers take the professional approach and fill the page with words. It is okay if you do not possess professionally designed stationery; MS Word provides several versions appropriate for your use, or you might choose to type a single-spaced query letter the old-fashioned way, on a blank sheet of 8.5" x 11" white paper. But, in this rapidly advancing technological age, most query letters are submitted online or via email; however, if a literary agent asks for a hard copy, submit it that way.

If your manuscript is rejected, which often happens for most new authors, and you want it back, enclose a SASE. (A SASE is a self-addressed, stamped envelope, and this only applies to hard copies.)

If your query letter captures the attention of a literary agent, she will then request a copy of the whole manuscript. (See Appendix A for an example of a cover page (the first page) of a submission.)

Capture the agent's attention at the beginning of your letter with a rave review, an impressive sentence or two from your manuscript, a comparison of your writing style to a celebrated author's writing style, or a referral from one of the agent's clients. Some agents accept manuscripts only on referral.

Practice writing a condensed version of your biography. Do not overlook your academic and professional credentials and writing awards/contests. Your platform is essential, such as social media following, speaking engagements, membership in professional writing associations, and civic and community service. Some literary agents are impressed by an author's affiliation with a writers' conference—indicating your level of seriousness about your craft. And, whatever else you do, do not write in the negative, belittling, or self-effacing terms: "This is my first attempt at writing a book. I sure hope you like it." Instead, literary agents prefer to represent authors who believe in themselves, especially in their writing.

As for the synopsis, it must be concise and flow smoothly into the body of your letter, unless, of course, required as an attachment.

Be assertive. Show the agent how your story fits into a particular genre, such as children, YA/MG, women's fiction, romance, or suspense. Share data from your platform substantiating that assertion. Yes, to some extent, you assist the literary agent in doing her job. However, the more specific you are about your work, the easier it will be for the agent to move forward. (For a sample of one of my query letters, see Appendix B.)

Here, it is important to note that sometimes literary agents get it wrong; they misjudge or make an untenable assessment of an author's writing style and market potential. Specifically, I refer to a rejection of one of my manuscripts because the agent "did not like the quality of [my] writing." Shortly after that agent rejected my work—who, by the way, had initially expressed interest in it—I retained a hybrid publisher. Then I entered my novel in an international book contest and won the first-place category. (See Step Six: "Promote and Sell Your Book" in the section on Book Contests.) I believed in my work, and although I failed to land a literary agent, I kept searching for one, and I kept writing, too. Please do not become disillusioned in your search for a literary agent. Most of them are great at their profession, but none is omnipotent.

The *Guide to Literary Agents* also provides a glossary of industry terms that most emerging authors will appreciate learning. Success stories about authors who landed their prized literary agents are woven throughout the guide, as are stories by literary agents bragging about their accomplished authors. This reference tool also addresses best practices, such as acquiring licensing for subsidiary rights, quotation rights, anthology, translation, English language reprints, mechanical reproduction, electronic/software, sound broadcast, film, television/reading, non-commercial, dramatization, documentary, merchandising, audiobook, performance, and much more.

Another practical resource is *Writer's Digest*, a must-have reference tool for all writers. The digest provides information about writing competitions, publishing in all formats, submissions, and proposals, writing query letters, success stories about literary agents and authors about how they ended up doing what they do, and more. It also offers creative writing tips (prompts) and advice about writing fiction.

Two other resources are *Writer's Market* and *Novel & Short Story Writer's Market*, the go-to reference tools for writers interested in learning about where and how to sell their work: articles, books, fillers, gags, greeting cards, fillers, novels, plays, scripts, and short stories. For example, *Writer's Market* contains an abundance of information about publishers, small presses, book packagers/producers, consumer publications/consumer service/business opportunity, detective/crime, disabilities, entertainment, ethnic/minority, food/drink, games/puzzles, general interest, health/fitness, history, hobby/craft, home/garden, humor, in-flight, juvenile, "little"/literary magazines, men's, military, music, mystery, nature, conservation/ecology, personal computers, photography, politics/world affairs, psychology/self-improvement, regional (broken down by states), relationships, religious, retirement, romance/confession, rural, science, science fiction, sports, teen/young adult, travel/camping/trailer, fantasy/horror, women's, trade/technical/professional journals, advertising/marketing/PR, the gamut. Scriptwriters might appreciate the business and educational writing sources, playwriting, screenwriting, and numerous other fields. There is also a glossary of terms most emerging authors would find helpful as they continue navigating all that the publishing realm provides.

Like the other two reference tools previously mentioned, *Writer's Market* and *Novel & Short Story Writer's Market* provide literary agent contact information and submission requirements. But they also show authors how to access consumer and trade magazines and the contests and awards related to those media. The latter provides aspiring and accomplished authors with much information about getting published and navigating the industry. Both volumes are practical resources.

Of course, there are other reference resources; but I find these four the most practical. And although they offer seemingly similar information and services, each is unique in its own right.

There is one other task that all authors must undertake: retaining the appropriate legal counsel. Nearly all best-selling and celebrated authors will attest to this necessity. Some might even acknowledge some of the pitfalls they encountered along the way when they did not have such a relationship. While producing this handbook, several accomplished authors shared stories with me about what happened to them because they did not realize they should have consulted an attorney *before* signing their publishing contracts. Like many aspiring authors, these authors were "simply thrilled" to get their work published. Unfortunately, in nearly all the cases involving these authors, their books are selling, but they, the authors, are not benefitting financially. For sure, obtaining legal counsel is something to consider.

Retain a Contract Lawyer or an Intellectual Property Rights Attorney

As noted earlier, some authors search endlessly for a literary agent not only to sell their manuscripts to a traditional publisher but because of their expertise in reading and interpreting publishing contracts, which reduces the need for *a contract lawyer* or *intellectual property rights attorney.* However, unless the literary agent is also an attorney in one of these fields, I prefer to err on the side of retaining independent legal counsel as well. Besides, the agent already possesses an undeniable bias in her relationship with the publisher; this is not to imply she does not operate in her client's best interest. Yet, the necessity of retaining legal counsel cannot be overstated. So, before signing a contract—or anything else, for that matter, with a literary agent, a hybrid, or a traditional publisher—consult an attorney.

Since I am an indie author and self-publisher, I do not have a literary agent; I represent myself, but not without legal counsel. One time, I received what read to me like a great offer from a universally recognized hybrid publisher to publish one of my novels. First, I conferred with two of my trusted colleagues (who are themselves published authors), after which I then contacted my family attorney who, in turn, referred me to a contract attorney, who, in turn, read and interpreted the multi-page document for me, as I summarize below:

> "Before you sign this *contributory* contract, you should know at least three things: First, you are paying them to publish your book with no guarantee of sales.
>
> "Second. Say your book turns into a blazing success. You will be granting the publisher all the rights outlined in this contract—including all the subsidiary rights—for however long the publication lasts, which could extend beyond your lifetime."
>
> Then he was more positive when he said, "Although this is a hybrid publisher, for whatever reason, they're offering you more than double the typical royalty rates offered by traditional publishers, *and* the portions for the gross proceeds for the subsidiary rights are equally competitive as well."
>
> With an air of finality, he concluded: "If you like, we can try to negotiate some of the subsidiary terms. The choice is yours."

He did not say, and I already knew—that publishing contracts are virtually ironclad, hardly ever negotiable. But one never knows unless she tries to negotiate some of the terms and conditions, especially if the author is a best seller of the magnitude of the likes of Agatha Christie or J. K. Rowling. Negotiation is even more to an author's advantage when movie rights are at stake *if* an offer for movie rights follows the original contract signing—i.e., there was no subsidiary clause granting movie rights in the first place—which is highly unlikely.

Although the attorney was much more detailed than what I present here; still, I believe you get the main point about the need for legal counsel. As it so happened, I had a crucial decision to make. In contrast to my relationship with a lesser-known hybrid publisher some time ago—who offered no clause of discontinuance of publication nor anything about promotion services and royalties, and there certainly was no mention of subsidiary rights—save for the contributory clause, the more reputable hybrid publishers operate more along the lines of a full-service publishing house. Also, in contrast, after the lesser-known hybrid publisher finished their part of the contract, they turned over all the publishing rights back to me, the author, thus ending our contractual relationship. But I was then on my own to market, promote, and sell the book, not to mention converting it into other formats, such as a hardcover and an e-book. Do not assume that all hybrids operate similarly to a full-service publishing house. Do your homework. For a certainty, they have done theirs on you.

Bottom-line: it would be wise to retain legal counsel *before* entering what you think is a good deal with a literary agent, a hybrid publisher, or a traditional publisher.

At this point, you might be thinking, *I had no idea there was this much work in getting published.* Well, there is, and there is more work ahead if you truly desire to get published.

So, let's get published. Part II of this handbook assumes that your manuscript is ready for publication.

Part II:

Self-Publishing
Your Way

Part II of this handbook covers the final four steps: the publishing essentials—of which there are many—including formatting a book, converting an MS Word document into digital and e-book files, uploading files onto the print-on-demand and distributor websites of your choice, promoting, and selling books, and creating your own roadmap.

This part assumes the author has a completed manuscript and that it is ready for publication.

Instructions are provided in intricate detail, from obtaining a professional headshot, professional name, employer ID, incorporation, permission rights, copyright, ISBN, pricing, distributors, metadata, and BISACs to creating a domain, website, and a landing page, among other publishing essentials.

Then there are the technical procedures for the conversions, mainly book formatting, MS Word document conversion into ISO-validated digital and e-books, as well as submitting these files to your on-demand printer and distributor for printing, distribution, and sales.

After getting published—to bring attention to your books—authors must actively promote them.

As I mentioned in the Preface, eventually, whether you publish your work yourself or retain a hybrid publisher, or search for a literary agent, there is nothing more empowering than knowing that you can publish your work yourself. Either way, I am reasonably sure something inside these pages will be advantageous in your quest to become an accomplished book author, maybe even an accomplished indie publisher!

Finally, authors are encouraged to modify the rules and steps in this handbook to suit their own situations.

For now, let us turn to Step Four - the publishing essentials.

Step Four: Getting Published - The Essentials.

Getting published is comparatively more straightforward than pretty much all else discussed in this handbook.

As we advance, everything else you do will reflect on how people see you, including your name, picture, the content of your book, book title, cover, website, et cetera. Think PROFESSIONAL IMAGE, QUALITY, and PRESENTATION.

What impression do you want to project, particularly with your book cover? Start by getting *a professional headshot*. The top-far left photo is a decade old from my twenty-fifth wedding anniversary. It was never intended for public display, but I used it in each of my novels published to date. The photo top center is even older. The picture top-far right and the one on the second row are of me, M. J. Simms-Maddox, in 2021.

My advice: get a variety of pictures for different uses. The pictures should be three to five years within your current age to be recognized for who you are now.

Create a **professional name** (a *pen name* or a *pseudonym*). By what name do you want your work to be published?

Obtain an *Employer Identification Number* (*EIN*) at www.irs.gov/businesses/small-businesses-self-employed/employer-id-numbers. Remember, you are operating your writing career as a business, even if you are its only employee. Your accountant can help you with this.

Incorporate as an *Inc.* or an *LLC.* or as another type of corporation in your state. Remember: it is vital to protect against claims and lawsuits, not to mention the appropriate way to file taxes. Either your accountant or your attorney can help you get incorporated.

Before copyrighting your work, double-check for copyrighted material you may have used inadvertently in your manuscripts, such as text, data in charts, artwork, images, or graphics. If you did not create any of that material, odds are it is copyrighted by someone else. If so, you need to acquire *permission rights* to use that copyrighted material.

A Word about Permission Rights

Obtain *permission rights* from copyright holders and publishers whether using the artwork, text, or the graphics from the copyrighted material, which includes books, magazines, newspapers, reference journals, such as *The Chicago Manual of Style,* lyrics from poems, speeches, and songs, and information obtained from the internet and websites (Consult the *CMS* 2017, sections 4.75 and 4.76, p. 207 for further information.)

A hard-learned lesson. Some time ago, I authored an op-ed article about Robert Mugabe's resignation from the presidency of Zimbabwe. A newspaper published my article and used a photo of the subject. But it did not occur to me that the publisher then held the copyright to my article, not to mention permission rights to the image. Meanwhile, I copied the photograph from the news article online and posted it on my website. Several months later, I received a letter from a law firm representing the photographer notifying me that I had used the image without the photographer's permission. The correspondence also noted the start date of my use and charged me over $400.00. I should have known better because it was a reputable news source. So, whatever you do, never cut and paste anything from the internet onto your website unless, of course, it is advertised as a "free download." If it is not your material, find out who owns it and obtain permission to use it. Since most permission requests are made online, see Appendix G for an example of information that copyright holders and publishers typically request before granting permission rights. Obtaining permission to use portions of or whole copyrighted materials can be daunting and expensive too. But, if you can navigate the websites of the Copyright Clearance Center, the U.S. Copyright Office, or the respective publisher's website, no problem.

You might be surprised to learn that some copyright holders prefer to see how their material will appear in your publication.

As for turnaround time, three months elapsed before I obtained permission rights for copyrighted material for *Their Eyes Were Watching God*. In early December of 2020, I began preparing and eventually mailed a letter requesting permission rights to excerpt the book's first three pages; two months lapsed, and no word. So I chanced to explore the Copyright Clearance Center, clicked on the "Help" tab, and learned that the book has a different publisher than the one cited on the copyright page of the edition that I possess. I submitted a new request online; another month passed. Then I received a text message, followed by a telephone call from a permissions officer at HarperCollins Publishers. Polite and informative, the officer explained the costs associated with print runs, about which I was wholly unfamiliar. After helping me streamline my request, the officer sent me a contract allowing ninety days to respond. My permission rights to use the first three pages of *Their Eyes Were Watching God* cost $195.00 for a print run of 1,000 for five years. However, if I sell this handbook in the United Kingdom and the British Commonwealth, I must obtain permission from Little Brown and Company Publishers in the United Kingdom. At this point, I am thinking; *You have got to be kidding me*. Had I consulted *The Chicago Manual of Style* earlier, I might not have been shocked.

Obtaining permission rights and costs vary.

I contacted the permission rights officer at another publishing house to use fourteen pages of *Black Professional Women in Recent American Fiction*. I received a response within one week. There was no elaborate contract, no time constraint, and no print run stipulation, merely the following:

> Permission is granted to use the material on pages 151-162, 165-166, and 170 as requested. Please abide by the following:
> - One-time non-exclusive use only.
> - A fee of $500.00, payable to McFarland & Company, Inc.
> - Use the following credit line: From *Black Professional Women in Recent American Fiction* © 2004 Carmen Rose Marshall by permission of McFarland & Company, Inc. Box 611, Jefferson NC 28640. www.mcfarlandbooks.com.

Oh, but had my subsequent request happened as smoothly as the first two. All efforts to locate the copyright holder *and* the publisher of Jessie Rehder's *The Young Writer at Work*—the primary source for the creative writing standards used in this handbook—were unnerving. I should have known something when it became clear that the book was no longer in print. Originally published by The Odyssey Press, Inc. in 1962, the edition that I possess is the seventh printing and was published by The Bobbs-Merrill Company, Inc. in 1977. Meanwhile, Bobbs-Merrill was acquired by Macmillan, where the permission rights officer with whom I communicated noted, "The current iteration of Macmillan did not acquire many (if any) Bobbs-Merrill titles." She also referred me to Prentice Hall/Pearson and PLSclear, where the permission granting analyst noted, "Not a Pearson publication... Please contact the relevant rights holder for permission."

I Googled the author's name and the book title again and came across J Merrill Publishing, which, from all indications, appeared to be a hybrid publisher. Still, I submitted an inquiry, but to no avail.

I contacted the U.S. Register of Copyrights—where I was confident that I had already investigated—and prayed that the book was in the public domain, not to mention that fair use applies. Instead, I received a response regarding fees for conducting a manual search starting at $200/hour for an estimated two hours or more: "Please note, few of our searches can be completed in two hours. If additional fees are necessary to complete the request, we will communicate with you and payment can be rendered at that time…," which, I estimated would be far more expensive than the permission rights.

I contacted Jessie Rehder's long-ago employer—the Department of English and Literature at the University of North Carolina at Chapel Hill—who, apart from recommending many of the steps that I had already taken, also suggested I consult a copyright attorney.

I then learned from a copyright attorney that there is no record in the Copyright Office Public Catalog of Rehder's *The Young Writer at Work*. Yet, it is possible that she never even registered copyright, albeit copyright could exist without the benefit of registration in the Copyright Office. It is also possible that Rehder bequeathed her copyright(s) to her heirs as part of her residual estate and that they might not even be aware of this.

Toward the end of my search for the copyright holder of the Rehder book, I remembered *The Chicago Manual of Style* covers this issue in the section on "The Author's Responsibilities: the missing copyright owner" (The *CMS* 2017, section 4.82, pp. 209-210). Since I had already followed all the "reasonable" steps to locate the owner, I ended my search. Yet, I mention my "reasonable efforts" on the copyright page of this handbook in the event an owner surfaces and levels a claim against my corporation. At the least, I can document my good faith efforts to locate the current copyright holder and compensate her for using the material. Indeed, something like this has happened to someone other than me.

Notice the many references to permission rights throughout this handbook. Even after paying for permission rights, authors must also acknowledge the use of the copyrighted material on the copyright page, the acknowledgment page, and in the footnotes of our work. I even include them in the References.

Obtaining permission rights to use copyrighted material is another reason some authors seek hybrids or traditional publishers. Regardless, publishers typically hold the authors responsible for fees (or a portion). So, either way, the author pays for permission rights. In some instances, though rare, there is no financial cost. For example, if an author wishes to cite a literary work or a sentence or two, the copyright holder merely requests that the author cites "By Permission of the Publisher."

My advice: unless the copyrighted material is essential, find another way to make your point.

After exhausting all reasonable efforts to obtain permission rights—if applicable—authors may apply for, purchase, and assign *copyright* to their work—for example, ©2019. (See the copyright page to this handbook). Meanwhile, protect your intellectual property—copyright everything—even poorly written drafts. Doing so is your primary protection, if not the only defense, against someone else claiming and profiting from your work—speeches, PowerPoint presentations, poems, scholarly papers, short stories, book-length manuscripts, audio/video productions, everything.

For work produced after 1977, the copyright extends throughout the author's life plus seventy (70) years. So the question then arises, "Who benefits after that time?" For copyright renewal, you might consider bequeathing your copyright(s) to heirs as part of your residual estate. You might also add someone else's name to your copyright. For example, Zora Neale Hurston's *Their Eyes Were Watching God* and J. R. R. Tolkien's *The Lord of the Rings* trilogy, both list additional copyright holders. Whether Hurston and Tolkien added those names themselves is beside the point, especially since copyright law allows the extension of the rights to surviving spouses, children, and other heirs. Copyright law is complicated, which is another reason that authors should retain legal counsel. Even so, would you not want a family member or some other loved one to benefit from your success as an author? Otherwise, the latest publisher, which might be a different imprint, would most likely benefit. Think about this carefully. For more information, consult a copyright attorney and sections 4.19-4.33 on "Copyright and the Public Domain" in the *CMS*, 2017, pp. 178-183.

To apply for a copyright, proceed as follows:
- ✓ Go online to https://www.copyright.gov/registration.
- ✓ Sign in or register for an account.
- ✓ Scroll down to "Literary Works."
- ✓ Look for "Electronic Copyright Office."
- ✓ Select "Registration System (eCO)."
- ✓ Select "Preview standard application to Register Literary Work."
- ✓ Complete the form and then submit it. There is a fee for this service.

Then, register an account and apply for a Library of Congress *preassigned control number* (*PCN*)at https://www.loc.gov/publish/pcn/ *before* your book's publication date. Select the "PrePub Book Link" and complete the form in the "Author/Self-Publishers Portal." Librarians use the PCN to catalog books, for example, fiction or poetry. A PCN is also an added layer of protection; insert it on the copyright page of your book. There is no fee for this service.

Upon publication of your work, send two (2) copies (called "mandatory deposit") to the U.S. Library of Congress at the following address:

      Library of Congress
      Copyright Office
      Attn: 407 Deposits
      101 Independence Avenue, SE
      Washington, D.C. 20559-6600.

This action verifies author ownership of the copyright and should be transacted within three (3) months after the work is published. There is no fee for this service.

Write a concise **biography**. (See "About the Author" at the back of this handbook. A version of fewer words is usually placed on book covers, dust jackets, or in the Back Matter.)

Write a *blurb* or *hook* (not the synopsis of your book) to pique readers' interest. Consider excerpting a compelling scene and inserting it on the back cover of your book. You might even have an excellent review suitable for promotional purposes; use it. (See a sample of a back book cover of one of my books in Appendix E.)

Purchase and assign an *ISBN* (International Standard Book Number) and a *price barcode* to your book(s). (Assignment is usually done during the conversion process, which follows this step.) Bowker provides these 13-digit numbers; for example, 978-1-7322406-6-7 was assigned to one of my books. The ISBN identifies and tracks books published in the United States. Register this number with your distributor and insert the number on the copyright page of your book.

   ✓   Go online to www.Bowker/IdentifierServices.com.
   ✓   Sign in or register for an account.
   ✓   Scroll down to "ISBN International Standard Book Number."
   ✓   Select "purchasing."

(You may also purchase the copyright and a price barcode from Bowker.)

$34.99
ISBN 978-1-7322406-6-7

53499>

9 781732 240667

Shown to the left is an ISBN and a price barcode for one of my books. (Appendix E shows where an ISBN and a price barcode appear on the back of a book cover.) I find it practical to purchase a package of ISBNs and price barcodes because I publish my books in different formats: paperback, hardcover, and e-book. A packet of these items is also practical since separate ISBNs and price barcodes are required for each book's format. You can only use one ISBN for each format. Put another way: although it is the same title, you need an ISBN *and* a price barcode for a paperback, another ISBN and another price barcode for a hardcover, and yet another ISBN and yet another price barcode for an e-book, and so forth.

As alluded to above, price barcodes link automatically to the preexisting ISBN for your book. And although the two items are purchased separately, the price barcode connects automatically to the ISBN, resulting in one unit. Without a price barcode, buyers have no notion of the book's value.

> Always assign a price to your book; never say, "I'll take whatever you think it is worth." Recall Nettles' proclamation: "Forget the starving artist. Be the *thriving* artist."[9]

While on the Bowker website, be prepared to enter information about yourself and your books, such as the sole contributor (author), other contributors, artists, and illustrators, a succinct description of the book, a biography, the copyright date, the Library of Congress PCN, the anticipated publication date, and the book's *price*. It is also essential to identify your *target audience*—for example, YA/MG, College, and Trade.

Bowker offers other publishing services, especially for self-publishers, such as *Book2Look Biblet* and *ScoreIt™*; the latter compares your writing style with authors that match yours. I do not care for *Book2Look Biblet* because authors are expected to provide too much content for prospective buyers to make a purchasing decision.

---

[9] By permission of the author, James P. Nettles.

But I highly recommend getting a *ScoreIt*^{TM} analysis of your writing style. Later, in Step Six: "Promote and Sell Your Book," I illustrate how this analysis works in "Whose Writing Style Does Yours Match?" Bowker also provides electronic forms for press releases and sell sheets, marketing consultation and social media consultation, ways to pitch your story to the entertainment community, along with QRPlus codes, and more, all for a fee, of course. We turn now to "A Word about Pricing."

A Word about Pricing

Authors must pay serious attention to the value of their work, whether hardback, paperback, e-book, or audiobook. How knowledgeable are you about your book's subject matter? Have you considered the untold hours and other resources that it took to produce the final product? Does the book's price cover the costs of printing, sales tax, and distribution fees? Prospective buyers view pricing as an indication of worth. Know the value of your books, and price them accordingly.

What else is meant by pricing? It is one thing to assign a price to your book, typically set in U.S. dollars. It is another thing to earn comparable value for the U.S. dollar in another currency. For example, say your book retails for $19.95; we are, of course, implying U.S. dollars. To make this discussion easier, round off that figure to USD 20.00. Already you might be asking, "Where'd the dollar sign go?" When using the acronym USD, you have included the dollar sign.

Now, let us review the issue of foreign currency equivalencies to USD 20.00. Refer to Table 1, which shows the U.S. dollar's equivalency to four different currencies in early December 2020.

Table 1: Comparisons of the U.S. Dollar to Four Other Currencies *

United States	United Kingdom	Australia	European Union	Canada
US	UK	AUD	EU	Can, C, CA, or CAD
$1.00	£.75	$1.34	€.75	Can1.28
$20.00	£ 15.00	$27.00	€16.50	Can$26.00

*Currency exchange rates shown in this table are correct as of noon EDT, December 7, 2020. Exchange rates vary throughout each day and may reflect the U.S. dollar differently at the time when someone from another country purchases your book.

Do you notice anything peculiar about the information shown in Table 1? Although two currencies—the pound sterling and the euro—appear less in value than the U.S. dollar, it takes fewer pound sterling and euro to buy one U.S. dollar. Conversely, it takes more U.S. dollars to buy the pound sterling and the euro. Therefore, to make a profit, at minimum, authors must sell their books to the British and the European Union markets at a relatively higher retail price, 25% or more. So, instead of the retail price of USD 20.00, you might consider USD 25.00, even higher. Meanwhile, I am uncertain about how the BREXIT impacts all of this.

A hard-learned lesson. For nearly five years, I sold books at USD 20.00 in the United States and other countries, such as the United Kingdom, Australia, Canada, and those comprising the European Union, where the euro is used. But I never asked anyone—nor did anyone ever share with me—how pricing works in the global network. I was essentially giving away my books. I know this reads strange, but we must be ever mindful of the U.S. dollar exchange rate compared to other currencies, especially those worth more than the so-called Almighty Dollar.

On the other hand, Table 1 also shows that it takes more Australian and Canadian dollars to purchase American dollars: AUD1.34 and CAN1.28. Therefore, the book's retail price of USD 20.00 will yield higher profits in those two markets. But this discussion is only relevant as of noon on December 7, 2020, the day of reporting those exchange rates.

Upon entering the price of your book on your distributor's website, the currency is automatically converted into global currencies. However, as exchange rates vary, so, too, do the net profits for your book sales. You might need to rethink the price of your book(s). I have. Unfortunately, when the U.S. economy shifts downward, so, too, does the value of the U.S. dollar. For instance, when one of my books registered *a net profit loss*, my distributor recommended increasing the book's price for the country where the U.S. dollar had fallen. Even though you might not have time to follow the market reports, it will surely not hurt to periodically check your book sales status. Australia is a prime example where the U.S. dollar often falls short of generating a net profit. Unfortunately, pricing is another reason that some authors choose hybrids or wait until they get picked up by a traditional publisher.

Back to more publishing essentials. Select a *distributor* or more than one. I mostly use IngramSpark for my printed books and PublishDrive for my e-books. Other distributors include Apple, BookBaby, Google Play Books, Scribe, FindawayVoices (for audiobooks), ACX, Amazon's Audible and Kindle, Blackstone Publishing, Libro.fm, Bookshop.org—which targets independent bookstores—and IPG Publishing. Choose the ones that best suit your situation.

On the same site where authors upload their PDF/X compliant text and cover files (which we discuss in Step Five: "Convert Your Manuscript into an ISO-Validated Digital Printing File"), Bowker, IngramSpark, or whichever distributor, asks for a lot of information about the author and the book under the label, "New Title." These data are collectively called *"metadata,"* that is, the ISBN, the PCN, the book's price, full and short descriptions of the book(s), awards and reviews, the author's biography, basic industry-standard codes (BISACs), and the like. You might already have uploaded some of this information onto the Bowker website, where you purchased and registered your ISBN and price barcode.

What are *BISACs*?
These are codes that define your work's scope—often referred to as genre and theme. The primary categories are juvenile literature (children and young adult) and adult literature (fiction and non-fiction). But these categories are broken down much further. Some delineations are listed below:

- o Children's literature, such as picture and storybooks, animal fiction, historical, fiction, and non-fiction.
- o Young adult (YA) literature, such as classic fiction, adventure fiction, short stories, and non-fiction.

- o   Adult literature, such as fiction (classic—written before 1945—and contemporary), action, coming-of-age, erotica, fantasy, history, mystery, poetry, romance, Sci-Fi, thrillers, suspense, and so forth.
- o   Adult non-fiction includes biography, memoir, business, education, history, lifestyle, politics, religion, and travel.

If these data have not already been automatically retrieved from Bowker, you might need to refine your target audience on the distributor's website. Do not dismay. There are drop-down boxes to aid in refining your selections.

My novels are YA and Adult fiction. The BISAC for three of my books is FIC031090, which signifies fiction/thriller/terrorism. These codes are utilized by librarians, retail merchants, and bookstore staff to catalog, shelve, and sell books. Since buyers often request "the latest book on action and adventure," "the latest book on terrorism," or "the latest romance novel," give serious thought to how you define your work. It took me several years to learn how to refine the description of my novels.

Take your time uploading the metadata. This information appears on the internet, at Amazon, Barnes and Noble, Target, Walmart, etc., and wherever else people Google your name and book title. Meanwhile, you can always fill in, save, and complete the forms at your leisure but *ahead* of the publication date. On the other hand, you can change the publication date allowing more time to complete these data. Then, after publication, you may routinely update the metadata, including the book's price.

Get acquainted with your distributor(s). If you have questions, contact customer service. Although I had difficulty getting someone on the telephone during the height of the COVID-19 pandemic, I received speedy responses to my emails. Distributors want your business, for they are fully aware that self-publishing is one of the fastest-growing sectors in the marketplace.

Also, once the distributor validates that the interior and the cover files meet international standards for digital printing and that you have completed the forms with the appropriate metadata, it takes over the final production and distribution of your book. (Step Five: "Convert Your Manuscript into ISO-Validated Digital Printing and Electronic Files" covers this process.)

Authors must also select a *digital* (an *on-demand printer*) and an *offset printer*. Your distributor is your primary on-demand printer, the site where you upload your PDF/X compliant files for the production, distribution, and selling of your book in all formats. Although my primary distributor is IngramSpark, I also use other on-demand printers. Shop around. Printing costs vary.

Prior to the pandemic, I could place orders for print runs of 100+ books with a one-week turnaround. But circumstances changed during the height of the pandemic; it sometimes took as long as one month to fill such an order. Furthermore, the situation worsened for me when a favorite offset printer ceased printing books altogether.

In offset printing, the inked image is transferred (or *"offset"*) from a plate onto a rubber blanket, then rolled onto paper, vinyl, or another printing surface. Specifically, if your printer mentions "plates" in setup costs, hers is an offset print shop. Unlike digital printers, however, offset printers are better equipped for the high-quality printing for commercial purposes, as well as for large book orders of, say, a print run of 1,000 or more.

In this era of rapidly changing technology, authors should also create a *landing page*, build a *website,* and obtain a *domain name.* I find it best to outsource the construction and maintenance of these projects to a web administrator. Also, if you are just getting started, keep your website simple and easy to maneuver. I use WIX.com at a nominal monthly fee. Nearly all authors promote and sell their books on their websites.

Think carefully about your domain name. I have two domain names: my corporate name and an easy-to-remember name—NovelsbyMJ.com. Remember, this is how people the world over will come to know you. Visit https://www.mjsimmsmaddoxinc.com, a.k.a., www.novelsbymj.com to see how my website is designed. But if you prefer a platform that allows for detailed images and much interaction, it might be best to choose one other than WIX. Remember: I am old-school and possess a relatively simple style.

Other platforms include, but are not limited to, Leadpages, WordPress.org, Squarespace.com, Concrete5.org, GoDaddy.com, and SilverStripe.org. (For more information about these and more, consult James Nettles' *Business Essentials for Writers: How to Make Money in an Ever-Changing Industry* (2019)).

> Never leave book sales entirely to others, not even to your distributor or your publisher. Develop an independent business account and a payment plan of your own.

Establish a *business bank account* and a *payment plan*.
Select a financial institution that caters to sole proprietors and small businesses because you might not have adequate funds to maintain a major business account during the early years. When I set out, I used funds from my day job to open and finance my business account. I kept and continue to keep receipts from pretty much everything related to my writing and publishing, including meals with buyers and hotel and travel to book events, stocking inventory for sales on my website, technology, supplies, everything. In this way, I have documentation of my work at tax filing. Although my early years produced modest income from speaking engagements and book sales, it was not enough to reconcile my investment in the business. Unless you are a best-selling author from the start, it takes a while to generate income adequate to sustain a full-time writing and publishing career. But if you are committed, you will find a way.

Again, I ask, "Does your book's price factor in your arduous work and expertise, printing, packaging, shipping, and handling costs? Or are such costs separate from your book's price?" Ignore people who encourage you to sell your books "on the cheap." Why bother putting your book on the market if you are not interested in recouping a net profit? Think about this carefully.

There is also the matter of *sales taxes*. In North Carolina, where I am incorporated, the sales tax is currently 7 percent.

With respect to *book sales*, PayPal has made it simple for people like me—who are not proficient in technology—to sell my books on my website, on social media, in retail outlets, in person, and to maintain sales records. PayPal offers "Buy Now" and "Add to Shopping Cart" buttons, suitable for selling my books. These features enhance secure purchasing on my website. I can also insert links to my social media and other affiliate sites, driving customers to my website, Amazon, Barnes and Noble, Target, Walmart, etc., independent bookstores, and other outlets that sell my books. Frankly, I use only the services that I understand.

Although *payment from book sales* with PayPal is instantaneous, the service provider holds income from sales transactions until the client transfers funds to her business bank account or uses the funds to cover costs for items, such as book orders, conference registrations, and exhibition fees, and other purchases. PayPal also provides invoices, customer contact and mailing information, shipping labels, and other information recognized as best business practices in accounting.

Since I also sell my books at book events, all net profits accrue directly to my corporation. So, I earn 100% net profit from these sales, and I receive email notifications from PayPal confirming each sale.

Invest in a card reader, which comes in handy at book events and wherever people approach you on the go. If possible, avoid accepting cash. Cash transactions often lead to unnecessary paperwork, and they are cumbersome at tax time. I find it more convenient to enter customer contact information on my iPhone at the point of purchase rather than completing paper receipts. Some of us are likely to misplace the paper receipts, anyway.

> Buyers at book events want easy access to the payment. Tapping or swiping a credit card reader can make the difference between selling a book or not. It is also essential to know the currency exchange rate to the U.S. dollar *before* transacting sales outside the U.S. And although some buyers prefer cash transactions, that is, hard currency, some countries, like Sweden—where this author exhibited at the 2018 BOKMÄSSAN—accept only credit and debit card purchases. So, a card reader is essential for business' sake.

Other payment plans and card readers include Apple Pay, Google Pay, Square, Stripe, Ingenico, Aloha Pin, and Clover Mini.

Deposit all revenue from book sales, speaking engagements, and other book-related events into your business bank account—for example, **Pay to the Order of Jane Doe, LLC**—not into your personal bank account. It might be advantageous to create a spreadsheet and post all financial transactions, e.g., personal, and external funds—loans from family and friends, even financial institutions—transferred to your business bank account. In so doing, you can cross-reference sales reports from your distributors, bookstores, and other sites that sell your books as well as expenditures, such as conference registration, printing, and professional services like artists and web administrators. All of this will come in handy at the tax filing.

As for income from online book sales, IngramSpark's Lightning Source Print on Demand (LSI POD) issues periodic Wholesale Compensation Reports and remits payments quarterly via direct deposit into the customer's bank account. This information helps me file my quarterly sales taxes, too.

As for remittance for book sales from bookstores, small shops tend to issue annual sales reports, along with a printed check, which authors must also apply to their sales tax filing.

Big bookstores, IngramSpark, and PayPal also offer tutorials and webinars about their services.

Bear in mind that being a good businessperson does not necessarily equate to being an accomplished author or self-publisher. So, take your time establishing your writing career and publishing your book(s). And whatever else you do, do not underestimate the need to retain legal counsel, open a business bank account, and pay your corporate and sales taxes.

We are almost done.

It is time to convert your edited manuscript into an MS Word formatted document and then to digital, electronic, and audiobook formats.

At this point, you might be wondering, "Why do all this work if I can submit my manuscript to Amazon or similar such sites and let them format my book for me?" Yes, you have that option. But have you done research on what it means to publish on those sites? For example, if you purchase your ISBN and price barcode from one of them, are you inadvertently granting them *exclusive rights* for the sales, distribution, and printing of your book? Can you sell your book elsewhere, or are you restricted to one of them, for example, Amazon? Recall my advice about having an attorney read publishing contracts before signing. The same holds true with Amazon and similar online retailers offering to publish your book.

In contrast, this handbook is for authors who desire to learn how to publish their work themselves. Besides, do you not want to know how to format your book, create your own book cover, et cetera? What happens if, in the future, you no longer wish to use Amazon or whichever publisher you are considering?

Notwithstanding, unlike the cookie-cutter versions offered online, this handbook shows authors how to convert an MS Word manuscript into a book format, digital, e-book, and audiobook *their way* and then successfully upload the files onto print-on-demand and *distributors'* websites *of their choice*.

Either way, it is your choice.

You may also opt to skip this section and proceed to Step Six: "Promote and Sell Your Book."

Step Five: Convert Your Manuscript into ISO-Validated Digital, e-Book, and Audiobook Files.

Save the original *edited* manuscript separate from the conversion process. This way, you can always make copies to restart the conversion without damaging or losing the MS Word document.

The Mechanics

Here, we describe how to convert an edited manuscript from its 8.5 x 11-inch double-spaced Microsoft Word document into a book format, a digital document, an e-book, and finally, a word about audiobook conversion. There are, of course, several software packages, such as Vellum (for production of print and e-books) and Scribus, and Atticus, all equally good for publication production. But I am familiar most with MS Word and Adobe Acrobat Pro, hence these instructions. If you already have a template for your book's layout, skip this part and proceed to the Front Matter.

Otherwise, if you have not already set up the framework or the template for your book, first, check that you are using an easy-to-read font, such as Times New Roman, and that the font size is set to no bigger than 12 points. Is your copy (text) double-spaced? If not, it should be.

As we begin, remember that *page layout* and *pagination* can create an aesthetic appeal for a book.
- ✓ Select Layout; then choose Size.

- ✓ From the dropdown menu, select More Page Sizes.

- ✓ Under Page Size, select Custom size. In the box to the right of Width, type 6" or 5"; and in the box to the right of Height, type 9" or 8". The sizes 6" x 9" and 5" x 8" are industry standards. (This handbook measures six by 9-inches; however, the trim size is your choice.)

✓ Select *margins*. Set your manuscript's left, right, and bottom margins at *.5* (one-half inch). I almost always set the top margin at one inch (1").

✓ Back in the Home menu, select Paragraph. Under General, select *left* for alignment and *body text* for outline level from the dropdown menu. Enter *'0'* for before and after spacing. Then choose *double-space* for line spacing.

✓ In the Special box, select *first line*, which is where you indent the paragraphs. Enter *.4* or *.5*, but no more than *.5*. (As a rule, I do not indent the first paragraph of the first section of my chapters. So, I click on *none* for the first paragraph in each new section or chapter. Then I select *first line* and indent the subsequent paragraphs. The choice is yours.)

✓ Remember to use the *page break* for new chapters. To use the *page break*, click on Insert; click on Pages to the left, and then click on *page break*. As a keyboard shortcut to make a page break, press Ctrl + Enter.

✓ Some authors create page layout and pagination at the start of their manuscripts. In contrast, others wait until they complete their manuscript before dividing it into sections and chapters and applying pagination. This process is something that each author must decide for herself. I find it easier to create headers and footers and paginate along the way.

Pagination

✓ Pagination is the process whereby authors divide their manuscripts into pages, each of which may contain headers and footers. It might take several attempts to create footers and headers in your preferred style. Do not dismay. There are several ways to create pagination. It generally takes more time and effort than most people anticipate to create the type of header and footer they prefer. For starters, create a temporary header, footer, and page numbering system to follow until you can devote attention to designing these parts precisely as you want them.

What follows is one of the most straightforward ways that I create pagination and headers and footers. Practice until you develop the style that suits your purposes:

✓ Click on Insert, then, Header. Use a blank one-column header; over "[Type here]," type your heading (that is, the title of your book—the short title of this book is *Creative Writing and Self-Publishing*—but without the quotation marks.

✓ Click on Design under the Header - Footer Tools.

✓ To insert page numbers, click on *Page Number* and indicate where you want to insert page numbers, such as Top of Page, Bottom of Page, Page Margin, or Current Position.

✓ Click on *Format Page Numbers*, where several options appear, such as 1 2 3, -1- -2- -3-, i ii iii, a b c (and so on). Click on the choice of page numbering that you prefer.

✓ Under Design Tools, you have the option to choose a *Different First Page* or Different *Odd-* and *Even-numbered Pages*. I prefer to display the page numbers in the footers, flush left on even-numbered pages, and flush right on odd-numbered pages. I also insert the title and my name in the headers on even-numbered pages and the chapter titles in the headings on odd-numbered pages of my novels. But how you design your headers and footers is entirely up to you. At the least, you should display the book's title and the page numbers. Because this is a handbook for authors, I show only the title and sections in the headers and the page numbers in the footers.

✓ Play around with the drop-down boxes to learn creative ways to format the pages and design the headers and footers differently on the *First Page* and the Odd- and Even-numbered pages. Notice Roman numerals on the Front Matter pages in this handbook. You may also opt not to show any page numbers on the Front Matter pages.

✓ Use the *Link to Previous* tab if you want to create a new section (chapter). First, click on *Page Break*. Then click on the (highlighted) *Link to Previous* tab to *disconnect* the header or footer from the previous chapter or section. If the new section or chapter you want has the same section number as the previous one, click on "yes" to disconnect the link. A new section number appears for the next section (chapter). Then type the information you wish to display in the new header or footer. Apply this process to paginate and create different headers and footers throughout the entire manuscript. It took me many trials to master this procedure.

✓ I prefer to display the sections or chapters and the book title in my headers. This chapter is entitled "Step Five: Convert Your Manuscript into ISO-Validated Digital, e-Book and Audiobook Files," but I use a more concise title in the header, "Document Conversions," to indicate ways to convert MS Word documents, and nothing more. The shorter title also helps users locate these conversion steps when flipping through the pages of this handbook.

✓ If you prefer to display the same information in the header and footer of each of the subsequent sections (chapters), disregard the *Link to Previous* tab and merely check to ensure continuity with pagination.

✓ Click on Close Header - Footer.

Noteworthy: Microsoft Word provides helpful tips for creating page layout and pagination. I find it practical to print the tips on "How to Create Different Odd- and Even-numbered Pages" and so on. Then I file the printed instructions and retrieve them whenever I produce a new manuscript. This practice is old-school, but it works for me.

Next, you get to determine the content of your manuscript. For starters, the Front Matter is typically single-spaced and varies according to an author's preferences.

The Content of Your Manuscript

Front Matter generally includes the following:
>Flyleaf
>Title page
>Copyright/ISBN/PCN/permissions page
>Foreword
>Dedication
>Acknowledgments (optional for the Front or Back Matter)
>Preface or Prologue
>List Charts, Tables, and Illustrations
>Table of Contents
>A blank page before Chapter One (This rule is particularly the case when producing a novel.)

(See Appendix C for an example of the Front Matter in one of my books.)

Not all authors use a paragraph or section divider in their books. I do. Pressing the "Enter" button and starting a new section in a chapter, or using asterisks, seems bland to me. Instead, I use simple artwork to divide or separate sections within the chapters in my books. Some graphic text or paragraph and section dividers come at a financial cost. See three examples that I use below:

Mystery in Harare: Priscilla's Journey into Southern Africa

◆ ◆ ◆

Three Metal Pellets

Special Envoy

Page one of Chapter One (*and page one of subsequent chapters*) does not contain a header or page number and starts about one-half of the way down an odd-numbered page. To create this—on the first page of the first chapter—select *Different First Page*. However, some authors and publishers no longer begin a new chapter on an odd-numbered page, a protocol of a bygone era, from which I only recently departed. Instead—in an age of conservation and eco-friendliness—if a new chapter starts on an even-numbered page, it stays on that page. Put another way: books have fewer, if any, blank pages. This handbook contains several pages without numbering because I treat the "Steps" like chapters, such as Step Four: "Getting Published – The Essentials" and Step Five: "Convert Your Manuscript into ISO-Validated Digital, e-Book, and Audiobook Files," and so forth, and because I have not completely transformed!

Back Matter (Include only if applicable to your book):
About the Author   Appendices   Bibliography   Glossary   Index
Epilogue   References

It might be advantageous to review the subsequent sections with your graphic artist/designer and your printer as we advance. To begin, it is always good to examine books that are similar to yours and that portray similar specs that you prefer, such as the following features:

    Trim size (6" x 9" or 5" x 8")
    Page layout
    Structure
    Color (Is any text, or are images, illustrations, or photos in color?)
    Black/White (The ink color for printing is black.)
    Paper stock—for example, 50# white or crème

Book Covers
Just as distributors provide specs for book interiors, so, too, do they offer specs and templates for book covers and dust jackets. But authors provide their own artwork, ISBN, price barcode, and text.

Do not skimp on the *presentation*. Design the cover to draw attention to the book, and make sure the title "matches" the book cover. Just as chefs prepare cuisine in fine dining establishments, so should an author design her book cover. In

Appendix D, the front cover of *Special Envoy: Priscilla Journeys into Arab Islamic Territory* portrays a woman garbed in Islamic attire walking toward a building amid a shadowy setting that resembles a casbah. Imagine your book on display at a bookstore. Would you pick it up? The cover typically sells the book.

The copy (that is, the text) on the book cover ought to read as concisely and interestingly as the novel's narrative. (See Appendices D and E for examples of a front and a back book cover for two of my books.)

An author's photo is optional. (Mine is shown in the back matter of this handbook, page 184.) However, the ISBN and price barcode must be easily discernable on the lower back cover.

The following illustration is a template for a hardcover case-bound book that I shrunk to fit this 6" x 9" page. Although the specs are illegible on this page, the *template instructions* are included in the download. Some standard specs and different types of book covers are listed below:

- Black/white or full color and bleed
- Matte or glossy

- Trade paperback typically involves adhesive binding, which comes in three forms: burst, notch, and perfect bound
- Hardcovers—for example, case bound and clothbound, with or without a dust jacket. (This handbook was printed in a case-bound hardcover.) Books may be Smyth-sewn or side-sewn together or bound with adhesive. Also, heavy gauze may be glued to the spine, among other specs. (Hardcovers consist of boards covered with colored cloth.) There are, of course, different types of hardcovers.

Save your Microsoft Word-formatted book and label it by its ISBN, for example, 9780578178998text.docx. for the interior and 9780578178998cover.jpeg for the cover. If, however, you have not yet purchased an ISBN, use a short title of your book. You can rename the files later. Now, proofread once more.

Of course, specs for color interiors differ somewhat from those for black-and-white interiors. Either way, most graphic artists/designers and printers are adept at complying with distributor submission requirements. But, just in case, the next section shows you how to download the submission specs for yourself.

At this time, we turn our attention to converting your MS Word-formatted document into a digital printing file.

Figure 7. AdobeStock_217409116

Before converting your MS Word-formatted document, *ensure that no privacy or security data exist in the file*, such as encrypted passcodes. Delete any data that are not meant for public consumption.

The Conversion Process:
Producing an ISO-Validated Digital Printing File

This part covers the conversion process for the black-and-white book interior (text) and the book cover, presumably in color. *Adobe Acrobat Distiller software is required.* PrimoPDF—also Mac- and PC-friendly—and Vellum and Scribus, work just as well. I use a PC and am more familiar with Acrobat Pro DC—hence these steps:

✓ Have you already purchased, registered, and assigned an ISBN and a price barcode for this version of the book? If not, this is the time to do so. (Refer back to Step Four: "Getting Published – The Essentials.")

✓ Label the two MS Word-formatted files by their title or ISBN— 9780578178998*interior*.docx and 9780578178998*cover*.jpeg and *save them as pdfs.*

✓ Open the ISBN*interior*.pdf. Proofread it. Does this version resemble what you want readers to see? Does it replicate the MS Word formatted document? If not, make the appropriate changes in the MS Word-formatted document and save it as a pdf again. The page count and layout for both versions should be the same. If not, check for blank pages in the pdf version. Delete the corresponding blank pages—often created by page breaks—from the MS Word formatted file. Additional pages might also appear if the artwork and other graphics are improperly placed into the MS Word formatted version; check that they are the same. Now save the file in pdf again.

Document Conversions

- ✓ When satisfied that the pdf version adequately reflects the MS Word formatted document, click on "File" and scroll down to *save as prepress*; select "*PDF/X.*" A spinning circle reveals *preflight* functions such as flattening, color, font embedding, and transparency. The preflight might take a moment.

- ✓ Select "Export."

- ✓ Select "More Formats."

- ✓ Select "Postscript," "Export," and then save the file on your desktop.

- ✓ Double click the postscript icon; Acrobat Distiller opens. A box with the word "Standard" appears. The program should be preset for *PDF/X-1a:2001* or *PDF/X-3:2002.* The International Organization for Standardization (ISO) runs and validates that the conversion meets universal digital printing standards. The process takes a few seconds and lets you know when it is completed.

- ✓ Save the newly converted PDF/X-1a:2001 compliant text file in a folder on another storage device, such as a thumb drive, and label the folder "Distiller Files."

- ✓ If you have not already registered for and opened an account with a distributor, now is the time to do this. (Return to Step Four: "Getting Published – The Essentials," such as IngramSpark, where authors log in at https://myaccount.ingramspark.com/).

- ✓ To generate a template for your book cover, select a trim size, 5" x 8" or 6" x 9" and, if the page count is an odd number, round it off to the nearest even number. Ask the distributor to email the cover template via https://myaccount.lightningsource.com/Portal/Tools/CoverTemplateGenerator. When applying copy and artwork, stay within the pink, blue, and white areas stipulated in the specs. Otherwise, your graphic artist can perform this procedure for you.

- ✓ Save the ISBN*cover*.pdf in the Distiller Files folder, as well.

✓ If you have not already done so, upload your metadata. Click on "New Title." One of the first items you must enter is the ISBN for your book.

✓ Now, enter the title. You will also be asked whether there is a subtitle.

✓ Completing the metadata takes quite a while. Dropdown boxes enable refinements, such as the genre and audiences. Take your time completing this section. You can always "save" and return later to edit and complete this information. Also, take care in selecting a publication date. If, at some point, you cannot complete and upload all of the metadata *ahead* of the scheduled publication date, *change the publication date to reflect a more realistic release date*. For example, change your publication date from December 20, 2022, to March 20, 2023.

✓ Select the specs for your book, that is, the trim size (6" x 9" or 5" x 8"), page count, format (hardcover, dust jacket, case bound, perfect bound (paperback), paper stock, and color, interior (color or B/W), and so forth.

✓ IngramSpark offers Print and E-book, Print, or E-book. Select whichever format suits your purpose. There is a conversion fee.

✓ *Noteworthy*: some distributors, such as IngramSpark, help build your book. Upload each part of your manuscript, such as the Front Matter, and then section by section or chapter by chapter. You need not fret about converting your MS Word-formatted document into a digital printing file alone. These instructions are for authors who want to learn how to perform the conversion themselves. Besides, you might prefer to create the book design and layout *your way*. For sure, you do not want your book produced from a cookie-cutter.

✓ Upload the distilled cover and text files to your distributor's website. The distributor will inform you of any problems with your files; fix them. Then upload them again. Mauve-colored warning messages might pop up. However, you can be reasonably confident they are due to variations in fonts, e.g., New Times Roman and Minion or whatever fonts you use, flattening, and low-resolution artwork. But if you have already utilized preflight and run the Distiller program, you need not worry.

✓ By this point, you can be reasonably confident the mauve-colored warning messages are due largely to variations in fonts, e.g., New Times Roman and Minion or whatever fonts you use. But if the message stipulates the artwork needs to be saved in a larger size resolution or somewhat differently, fix it.

✓ However, if you notice problems with the eproof and want to make revisions, you must first "approve" the eproof. Then edit and revise the MS Word formatted document and save it as a pdf again. Double-check that the pdf and the MS Word format are identical in page count, layout, pagination, and so forth. You must also perform the Distiller conversion again *before* re-uploading the revised files to the distributor's website.

✓ The distributor will then email you an eproof at no additional cost (or a hard copy at your request and usually for a fee for your approval via UPS or the USPS).

✓ *My advice*: always order a hard copy of print versions to see exactly how your book reads and looks. This way, you can edit and revise the content, and the cover, if necessary, and then upload the files again. Although there is a fee for this procedure, it is worth it.

✓ After reviewing the hard copy proof, you will be given several options, such as those shown below:
   o The customer approves this title (book) for printing, distribution, and sale from orders placed by her account and retailers.
   o The customer approves this title for printing from orders placed by her only.
   o However, if you do *not* approve the proof of your title (book), either you will be asked to upload revised content or explain the reason for your rejection.
Then, click on "submit."

When, finally, you receive an acceptable proof, you are done. Congratulations!

The conversion processes tend to cause some users anxiety. Do not forget the option of building your book on the distributor's website. But if you do not have the time or the desire to learn the mechanics of converting your document into a digital format, consult one of the hybrids or indie publishers and join a professional writers' conference. You might also consider enrolling in a computer technology course at the local community college to learn how to use Adobe Acrobat Pro DC, and other software packages, which simplifies the conversion process. *Besides, you don't want to miss out on publishing your book because you do not know how or do not wish to learn how to convert your MS Word documents into digital and electronic files*!

So, how did I learn how to convert my documents? A staffer at Adobe taught me in just a few minutes. I also benefitted from a virtual workshop conducted by a colleague in the North Carolina Writers' Network.

We turn now to e-book conversion.

> Be mindful that the electronic format might pose unforeseen problems, especially if you decide to grant subsidiary (licensing rights) to *a foreign publisher*. Also, since electronic distribution is challenging to limit geographically, this format is unattractive to foreign print distributors.

E-book Conversion

Some readers, primarily among the younger generations, prefer e-books because they are easily accessible on iPhones, tablets, and other electronic devices. E-books are also eco-friendly because the environment is comparatively less impacted than cutting down trees and making paper to print books. Regardless, some Baby Boomers, and others, too, prefer the look, feel, and smell of printed books, and lest we forget, their appearance on bookshelves in their homes.

Indies, hybrids, and traditional publishers have choices for e-book production. The PDF-based e-book best suits my preferences, so I use Adobe Acrobat Pro and Adobe Acrobat Distiller.

If you are a technophile and would like to produce a more elaborate version of your e-book, consider Amazon Kindle, DAISY (digital talking books), EPUB, or Microsoft Reader (LIT). These software packages can also convert your documents to XML and HTML source files.

- ✓ Have you already purchased, registered, and assigned a separate ISBN and a separate price barcode from your digital book for your e-book? If not, it is time to do so. (Refer back to Step Four: "Getting Published – The Essentials.")

Now, let us create your PDF-based e-book.

- ✓ You will need Adobe Digital, Kindle Previewer, or whatever app you use to read e-books.

- ✓ Is this a "New Title," that is, a different book from the one you converted to a digital printing file? If so, you must enter the metadata data for this new book. You can always "save" and complete the metadata section at your convenience. However, if this is the same title (book) that you recently converted to a digital file and selected Print *and* E-book during the digital conversion, you need not enter the metadata again because this is the same book; it is merely in an electronic format. Moreover, the conversion is automatic!

✓ Open a new folder and label it "E-book Files." If the digital and e-book are the same, download the EPUB and MOBI eproofs.

✓ Examine the eproofs with Adobe Digital, Kindle Previewer, or whatever app you use to read e-books. This step is perfunctory.

✓ You will then be given the same options to approve the e-book that you received for approval of the digital print format:
   o The customer approves the title (e-book) for distribution and sale from orders placed by her account and retailers.
   o The customer approves the title (e-book) from orders placed by her only.
   o However, if you do *not* approve the eproofs of your title (e-book), either you will be asked to upload revised content or explain the reason for your rejection.
   Then, click on "submit."

✓ When finally you receive an acceptable eproof of your e-book, download the EPUB and MOBI files into your E-book File folder. You are done. Congratulations! How simple that was!

✓ *On the other hand,* if you have not already converted this title into a digital version, refer back to the beginning in Step Five.

✓ This conversion is quick. There is a fee for this service.

✓ Open a new folder and label it "E-book Files."

✓ Locate the *PDF/X-1a:2001* or the *PDF/X-3:2002* compliant *text* file that you converted earlier and placed in your Distiller File folder. (See the previous section on converting MS Word-formatted files into digital printing files for details.)

Document Conversions

✓ Label and "Save" the *PDF/X-1a:2001* or the *PDF/X-3:2002* compliant *text* file with the new ISBN for your e-book.

✓ Save the ISBN*cover*.pdf in the Distiller Files folder, as well. Label and "Save" the front cover of your e-book the new ISBN and "save as" a 700-pixel jpeg in RGB.

✓ Upload the *PDF/X-1a:2001* compliant ISBN*text*.pdf and the ISBN*cover*.pdf (jpeg) to your *distributor's electronic book conversion* site.

✓ After uploading the two files, the distributor will inform you of any problems via mauve-colored warning messages; fix them, and upload the files again. However, if these are duplicate files that you previously used to create the digital documents, the conversion is virtually instantaneous and seamless.

✓ The distributor, in my case, IngramSpark, will email you an EPUB and a MOBI proof.

✓ Download the two eproofs. One is EPUB, and the other is MOBI.

✓ Examine the eproofs with Adobe Digital, Kindle Previewer, or whatever app you use to read e-books. This step is perfunctory as well because you have already performed the digital conversion.

✓ You will then be given the same options to approve the e-book that you received for approval of the digital print format:
   o The customer approves the title (e-book) for distribution and sale from orders placed by her account and retailers.
   o The customer approves the title (e-book) from orders placed by her only.
   o However, if you do *not* approve the eproofs of your title (e-book), either you will be asked to upload revised content or explain the reason for your rejection.
   Then, click on "submit."

When you finally receive an acceptable eproof of your e-book, download the EPUB and MOBI files into your E-book File folder. You are done.

Congratulations! Either way, you will have successfully converted your digital print version of the book into an e-book. How simple that was!

> A word of *caution*: Do not share your digital and e-book files with anyone other than your distributor and on-demand printer. These are your books!

A Word about Audiobook Conversion

Although this handbook is primarily about the "written word," some authors also desire to learn how to produce audiobooks. Moreover, many illiterate people enjoy listening to good storytelling and, lest we forget, the visually impaired. As for the conservationists and the environmentalists, audiobooks are produced in an eco-friendly medium.

I am least familiar with audiobook conversion of the three types of conversions, but I know enough to help get you on your way.

As with digital- and e-books, you must first purchase, assign, and register a separate ISBN and a separate price barcode for your audiobook different from your print and e-book.

Up to this point, we have been discussing and referring authors to print-on-demand and e-book distributors; however, the situation is different for audiobook conversion and distribution, and sales.

Specifically, authors first must find out which audiobook distributor, such as Audible Book Creation Exchange (ACX), Author's Republic, and Scribl and Podiobooks, publishes fiction vis à vis non-fiction books.

Once you have researched audiobook distributors, register an account with the distributor of your choice. Also, be prepared to upload the metadata about yourself as the author and your book.

Additionally, if you do not have access to audiobook software, such as Audible or Hindenburg[10], this is the time to make arrangements to use someone else's or purchase your own.

You might also find it practical to acquire a special microphone and a wireless keyboard to eliminate the clicking and typing sounds during the conversion.

- ✓ E-book conversion is the first step in producing audiobooks. If you have not already done so, convert the Distiller PDF/X text file into electronic form—that is, an e-book. (Refer to the two previous sections on digital and e-book conversion.)

- ✓ Even though the audiobook software provides detailed instructions, the conversion process is far more complicated than digital and e-book conversions. So you might opt to hire a professional narrator with access to a sound studio, especially if you have little patience or for some other reason.

- ✓ If you want to continue, dropdown boxes guide you through the process with instructions on doing pretty much whatever you wish, such as creating structure, recording, customizing styles, noise reduction, book export, et cetera.

- ✓ Open the file and click on "Start."

- ✓ Click "Open a new file."

---

[10] I learned about audiobook conversion during a workshop conducted by a Hindenburg representative during the Virtual 2020 Chanticleer Authors Conference.

✓ Click "Such-and-Such Book" (that is, the title of your book).

✓ The content is in e-book format. An EPUB or MOBI version of "Such-and-Such Book" automatically appears on the bottom half of the screen, making it easy for you to read.

✓ Play around with the tabs and remember: most software providers offer tutorials along the way.

✓ First-time users might find it best to begin at page one at the beginning of their book. Creating a "voice profile" and a cadence might take several readings. After finding your voice and rhythm, try reading a complete chapter. You can always edit.
   o Once a chapter has been completed, save the recording of it on one track.
   o Now, go to "Effects/Export."
   o Some alerts might appear; fix them.
   o Proceed to the next chapter, and so on, until you have recorded your whole book.
   o Click on "Export a book" to the distributor of your choice.

Granted, these instructions are a bit oversimplified. And although I might not have presented the whole picture, the purpose was to get you on your way. Even so, I am reasonably sure that all authors get the point that audiobook conversion is anything but easy.

Yet, if you completed all the steps and are reasonably satisfied with the quality of the audio version of your book, it is now available for distribution and sale!

As with digital and e-book conversion, if audiobook conversion is not something you want to do, it might be best to hire a professional narrator, or whichever distributor you use such as Amazon, Author's Republic, or Hindenburg to narrate and perform the conversion for you. But be ever mindful of inadvertently granting *exclusive rights* for the publication, distribution, and sales of your audiobook.

Limit sharing your audiobook. Audiobooks, like e-books, are copied easily.

Whichever format(s) you chose—if you successfully completed Steps Four and Five—you are now a published author!

In Step Six, we cover various ways to "Promote and Sell Your Book(s)."

Step Six:
Promote and Sell Your Book(s).

> Before spring 2020, book clubs, exhibitions, readings,
> signings at bookstores, and participation in professional
> development workshops were my best venues. But the
> COVID-19 pandemic forced me to learn how to engage
> virtually, primarily how to market and sell books online.
> It might take trial and error to determine which platforms
> work best for you, and I am still learning.

➢ **Promote, Exhibit, Travel, and Share News about Your Books.**
  - ✓ Whether this is your first or latest book, conduct a book launch
    around the time of its release. Consider venues like libraries, writers'
    conferences, bookstores, and colleges.

  - ✓ Consider using Pinterest to offer a unique author platform
    exclusively for your book(s). It is an image-sharing and social media
    service that many authors are gravitating toward. An excellent
    alternative or companion to Amazon and Facebook!

  - ✓ Donate (giveaway) items, such as books or pens, or notepads
    (bearing your name or book title), to book clubs, sororities,
    fraternities, the local Chamber of Commerce, Civitan Club, literacy
    agencies, creative writing classes, and women's crises centers.

  - ✓ Engage academic and local media—for example, newspapers and
    morning radio and TV talk shows. Apart from the *Salisbury Post*, I
    have also been featured in *Salisbury the Magazine*, *Senior Savvy
    Celebrating Life after 55*, and *Pebbles* (a Livingstone College newsletter). I
    occasionally write Op-Ed columns, too, such as the
    following:https://www.salisburypost.com/2008/01/13/whether-
    wind-or-wave-a-time-of-transition/ (The 2008 Presidential Election),

https://www.salisburypost.com/2011/08/14/my-turn-enigmatic-dysfunctional-washington/ (Deadlocked U.S. Congress), and MJ Simms-Maddox: Zimbabwe is reborn after Mugabe resigns - Salisbury Post | Salisbury Post (Implications of Zimbabwe President Mugabe's resignation). *(One of my strengths.)*

- ✓ *Arts and Sciences* (an Ohio State University alumni newsletter), https://artsandsciences.osu.edu/news-events/asc-spotlights/m-j-simms-maddox (Universities provide unlimited resources, especially for alumnae authors.)

- ✓ Exhibit your books at art festivals, book fairs, film festivals, theater festivals, retail establishments, churches, family events, schools, sorority/fraternity confabs, libraries, and the like, both at home and abroad. (*One of my strengths.*)

- ✓ Share information about your books on social media, e.g., Twitter, LinkedIn, Goodreads, Library Thing, Microsoft Teams, blogs, YouTube, ZOOM, Facebook, and podcasts. https://youtu.be/YgWfCrwtzec ("The Priscilla Series")

https://www.youtube.com/watch?v=jOeZk2LuGQQ (Meet the Author of Mystery in Harare)

- ✓ Learn how to use virtual event platforms, such as ZOOM, Socio, and Microsoft Teams; the latter is functional in countries and places that do not allow ZOOM.

- ✓ Share information about your books with state and national associations. The Women's National Book Association and the

North Carolina Writers' Network post "Hats Off!" "Shout Out," "Book Buzz," and much more about members on their websites. (*A weakness of mine.*)

✓ Travel. Take your show on the road, as it were. In the fall of 2018, I went on sabbatical to participate in the Harlem Book Fair, the South African Book Fair, the Bokmässan, and some smaller events back home. While on a flight out of Charlotte, North Carolina, to Sweden, I made an unexpected, resourceful acquaintance. The Charlotte Douglas International Airport is located near the Tryon International Equestrian Center. The annual TIEC had just concluded, and most of the passengers had participated in that event, one way or another. The "resourceful acquaintance" was the immediate past president of the International Association of Equestrian Journalists. I eventually told her about one of my manuscripts with scenes at the TIEC. My point is I met someone who could aid in the creation of plot about equestrian sports. But I would never have made such contact if I had not ventured into unknown territory. The "unknown territory" was the Bokmässan, and I eventually made contacts there, too. Traveling also broadens an author's worldview, providing exciting material for plot(s).

✓ Accept speaking engagements and book club presentations in-person and virtually.

✓ Participate in panels and roundtable discussions at writers' and related-professional conferences. (*Another of my strengths.*)

✓ Acquire an email list provider, such as MailChimp or MailerLite, and develop ways to engage readers. I created a monthly newsletter, "MJ's Outreach," encouraging followers to start writing, featuring new writers in each issue, and highlighting writers' associations and conferences. I offer copies of my novels and one-half-hour consultations on improving one's writing as incentives to respond to calls to action.

✓ Attend trade shows:
  o American Booksellers Association's Winter Institute
  o Book Expo America
  o Southern Independent Booksellers Association
  o New England Independent Booksellers Association
  o Great Lakes Independent Booksellers Association.

✓ The Frankfurt Book Fair, the London Book Fair, and the Sharjah International Book Festival are among the largest in the world.

➢ Participate in Book Contests.

State, national, and international authors' associations offer many opportunities for authors to participate in book contests. For example, as a member of the North Carolina Writers' Network, the Women's National Book Association, and the Chanticleer Authors Conference, I receive such notices year-round. Some competitions require a nominal fee for entry. Besides winning a contest or achieving an incredible status, you might also receive a book review, a ribbon, a plaque, or even a financial award. And much publicity comes your way, as well.

I entered *Mystery in Harare: Priscilla's Journey into Southern Africa* in the 2019 Chanticleer International Book Awards (CIBA) competitions. The novel advanced from a semifinalist to a finalist and to the Mystery & Mayhem Division's 1st Place Best in Category.

I entered another manuscript in the Carol Shields Prize for Fiction for women writers in the United States and Canada. My entry did not win the financial award, but it did capture the attention of someone on the editorial board. Now, I have a publisher, other than myself, for the fifth installment in the Priscilla Series.

Editorial boards for these high-level contests typically comprise well-known authors of the genre under review, acquisitions editors, librarians, professors, attorneys, corporate executives, officials from authors' and writers' associations, publishers (hybrids, indies, and traditional), and many other industry experts. Board members adhere to carefully constructed assessment criteria to judge entries for the various categories. Moreover, members serving on these evaluation teams know other professionals to refer to a promising author's work. For sure, they know what acquisitions editors are looking for in a manuscript. Just think, you might even get your manuscript read by a publisher, and by that point, the literary agents will come looking for you!

Are you interested in having your manuscript or book judged in a book contest? Here are a few more contests that you might consider entering:

the North Street Book Prize, the Nelligan Prize for Short Fiction, the Beverly Hills Book Awards, the Oscar Wilde Award, the Dzanc Books Prize, the INDIE Book Awards, the Next Generation Indie Book Awards, LitMag's Anton Chekhov Award for Flash Fiction, the Jeffrey E. Smith Editors' Prize, the New Letters Publication Award, and the Tom Howard/John H. Reid Fiction & Essay Contest.

Figure 8. Scenes from a book signing at the South Main Book Company, Salisbury, NC, Feb. 29, 2020. MJ joins Warren L. Bingham, center, author of *George Washington 1791 Southern Tours,* and Vincent Vezza, far right, regional rep of the Metro-North Region of the NCWN. Vincent's imprint is Hidden Treasure Novels (HTN) https://hiddentreasurenovels.com, derived from *The Hidden Treasure of Dutch Buffalo Creek* by Jackson Badgenoone (Vincent Vezza's pseudonym).

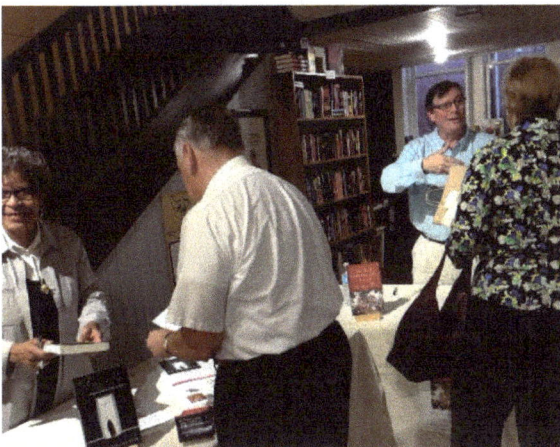

> ➢ **Join Professional Associations and Conferences.**[11]

CHANTICLEER
Int'l Book Awards
&
Reviews

Discovering Today's
Best Books!

WOMEN'S
NATIONAL
BOOK
ASSOCIATION

EST. 1917

African Literature Association

Connect
AAUW
OF NORTH CAROLINA

NC
WRITERS' NETWORK

---

[11] Permission granted to display logos by the respective organizations.

"The Writingest State in the Nation"

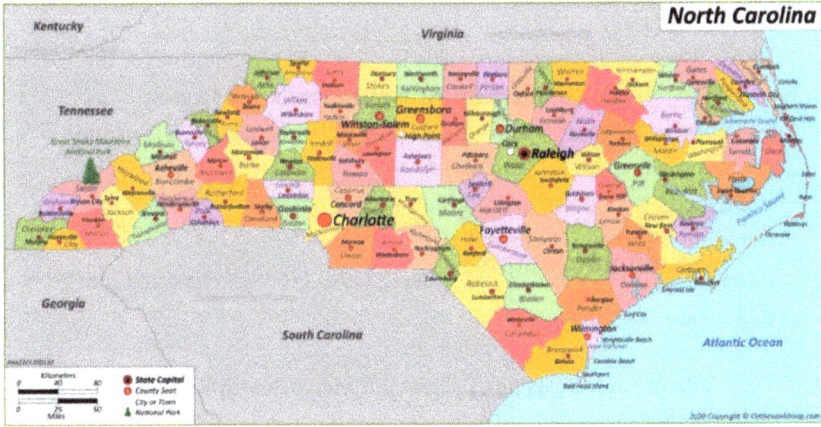

That North Carolina is "the writingest state in the nation" is debatable. However, this is but one of its claims, and I rather like it, too.

Are you affiliated with a writers' or authors' association or conference in your state? If not, now is a great time to join one.

Members of the North Carolina Writers' Network (NCWN) have access to loads of information and services, much of which I have yet to utilize. Nonmembers may visit the website at https://www.ncwriters.org/, but membership is required to access many of the links on display.

Although most of our meetings during the COVID-19 pandemic have been virtual, we in the Metro-North Region usually meet on the fourth Thursday in the early evening monthly at the French Express Coffee House in Kannapolis, slightly northwest of Charlotte. The ambiance is excellent, with warm and inviting staff, and an open yet cozy atmosphere. We pull tables together, order refreshments, take out our notepads and recorders, and speak openly, thereby allowing onlookers to listen to our discussion as well. Yes. We even buy one another's books!

The Metro-North Region members are fortunate for our insightful and vigilant regional representative, Vincent Vezza, who prepares agendas for our meetings, addressing the concerns and interests of the membership and keeping us abreast of significant changes in the industry. In an interview about resources for this handbook, he shared some information that emerging authors might find practical:

"It has been an honor to serve as a Regional Representative for the North Carolina Writers' Network. Our Metro North Region encompasses Cabarrus and Rowan counties just north of Charlotte and is home to nearly two dozen writers, many with at least one published work to their credit. For anyone interested in learning more about our authors, visit https://www.facebook.com/groups/1936971126391810/permalink/3749052871850284/."

Vincent also posts news about the Metro-North Region's membership on www.hiddentreasurenovels.com.

Ours is an active and diverse group of writers by age, ethnicity/race, socio-economic status, and occupation, and some are retired. Our genres, writing régimes, and inspirations for writing cover the spectrum. It is not uncommon for members to visit one another, share a meal, and confer about our writing experiences. Vincent is no exception. He visits members to see how we do what we do when we write, offers suggestions for improvement, and provides hands-on instruction to improve our use of technology. He is a vital link to the NCWN.

Members communicate with Vincent mainly on his blog, https://hiddentreasurenovels.com/blog, "which features initiatives launched by [his] imprint, Hidden Treasure Novels (HTN). One such initiative is a *Lessons Learned* playlist on YouTube, designed to provide a platform for sharing interviews with authors in the Metro-North Region and beyond." Watch Vincent's interview with author-entrepreneur Claudia Reuter, http://bit.ly/LessonsLearnedHTN.

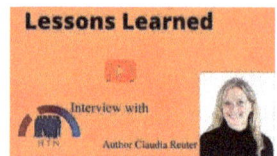

"During much of the COVID-19 pandemic, our monthly meetings have been conducted and recorded on ZOOM, with the consent of the membership, of course. After members introduce themselves, the guest speaker then has an idea about how to focus her presentation. Then we have a Q and A session." Vincent then makes the recording available to the membership, which is especially practical whenever we have special guests. I am most interested in the recordings on technology.

Vincent also "host[s] a column in a regional publication, *Senior Savvy Celebrating Life after 55*, which serves Cabarrus and Rowan counties. Titled *Trail Tales*, authors in the Metro-North Region typically submit 750-word articles or short stories." However, he stresses, "At HTN, we welcome authors from *and* beyond our region to submit their stories." I have submitted two articles and am always surprised when I meet people who say they have read them.

My interview with Vincent ended with him endorsing one of my stories: "We are pleased to have featured one of your stories, MJ, in the February 2020 issue entitled 'Share Your Dreams' on page 4, http://bit.ly/TrailTalesMJ."

Vincent is an accomplished author willing to work with authors at all levels and is tech-savvy too. So, one way or another, much of what the membership does gets pretty good exposure—primarily due to Vincent's marketing expertise. And this is just some of what the Metro-North Region membership receives.

But the most rewarding aspect of my membership is the valued relationships I make with other members. Why is that? More often than not, writing can be a lonely venture. But periodic association with like-minded people makes all the difference in the world; at least, for me, it does.

If you are interested in more information about writing opportunities in North Carolina, take a few minutes to explore the Metro-North Region website on Facebook and at www.hiddentreasurenovels.com.

And for more information about the NCWN, visit https://www.ncwriters.org/, and if you have questions, send an email to calendar@ncwriters.org. Hopefully, you will find each website informative, engaging, and impressive, offering something for nearly all writers and at nearly all levels, too.

The following are excerpts from the NCWN website[12]:

Publish
Find a call for submissions or a contest that's just right for you. Happy submitting! Please note: you must be logged in to see this page.

Need Feedback?
Use our Critiquing and Editing Service for professional feedback on your piece of writing. Only available to members of the Network.

Book Business Basics
If you're wondering, "How do I get published?" this exhaustive resource is the best place to start. Please note: you must be logged in to see this page.

Promote Your New Book
Did you just publish a book? Let us know and we'll post it in our Book Buzz section.

Share Your News
Do you have a reading coming up? Have you recently been published? Let us know so we can share it with all our members in our Weekly eBlast (for readings and events) or Hats Off! section (for all the other good stuff!).

Advertise
Get your book or service in front of people who will give you money for what you do.

Attend a Conference
Network members receive serious discounts on our three annual conferences.

---

[12] Permission granted by the NCWN to display data from its website.

Promote and Sell Your Book(s)

Find an Agent or Editor
Access our exclusive list of those <u>agents and editors</u> who have attended our conferences. Please note: you must be logged in to see this page.

Find a Job
Check out our listing of <u>jobs and residencies</u>. A new opportunity is right around the corner. Please note: you must be logged in to see this page.

Let People Find You
List your <u>blog</u> or <u>website</u> so your readers can find you easily.

Read Great Content
Not only will you now receive the *Writers' Network News,* but you can <u>access the *WNN* archives</u>. Please note: you must be logged-in to see this page.

Now that I have shared information about opportunities for writers in North Carolina, check out a few other scenes and ways that I promote and sell my books.
- ✓ Sometimes, readers ask for "mail-order forms" because they still make purchases with checks.
- ✓ Sometimes, readers call and purchase my books, similar to the way television shopping networks operate. I realize some of this is old-school, maybe even bazaar, save it is true.

Shown left are Angela Jacobs and Michael D. Connor proudly posing with MJ at her first book signing at Park Road Books in Charlotte.

MJ is joined by her sister, Jina McGriff, a graphic artist/designer, at the Harlem Book Fair.

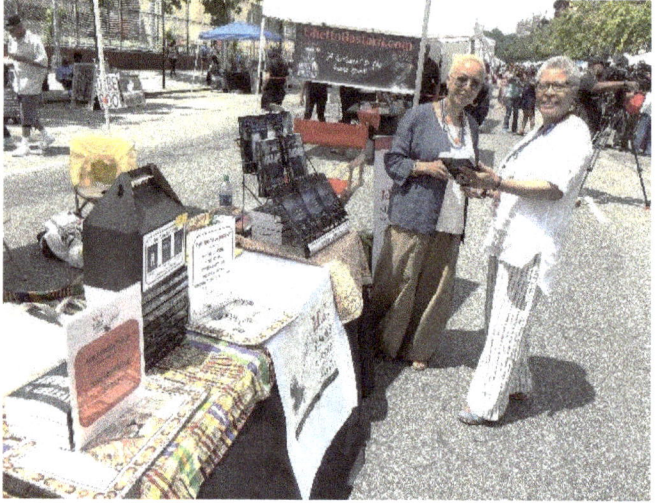

Delores Tyson, former President, and CEO of Planned Parenthood of Metropolitan New Jersey for 23 years, along with MJ in the center, and Lady Trisha Scipio, far right. Tyson and Scipio popped by to show their support of the author at the 2018 Harlem Book Fair.

Figure 9. MJ is amazed as she stands amid over 800 exhibitors at the Swedish Exhibition & Congress Center. Over 85,000 visitors attended over four days at the 2018 Bokmässan—the largest cultural event in Scandinavia.

BOKMÄSSAN
GÖTEBORG BOOK FAIR

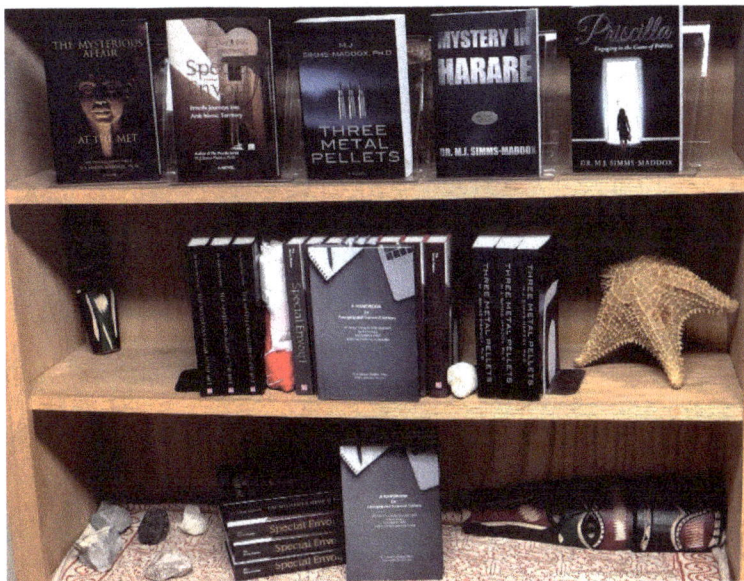

Figure 10. MJ and Elitha van der Sandt, Director of the SABDC, take a moment off from exhibiting at the 2018 South African Book Fair.

Hosting podcasts, selling online (e.g., Amazon, Barnes and Noble), social media, radio and television interviews, and virtual engagements, have become commonplace, however, authors of the old-school, myself included, continue holding fast to traditional ways of promoting and selling books:

- Getting books shelved at bookstores and doing readings and book signings, where proprietors and the author split the net profits at a ratio of 40-to-60 percent, respectively.
- Addressing book clubs and exhibiting at book fairs and comparable sites. (The reputable book fairs provide staff to manage sales, at a nominal fee, of course.)
- Some authors even make a practice of carrying books with them. One never knows when a fan or interested buyer will buy a book directly from the author.

Virginia Phiri is the 2021-2023 President-elect of the WOCALA-African Literature Association, a founding member of Zimbabwe Women Writers, and author of *Highway Queen, Grey Angels,* and many other novels. To her right is **Elinettie K. Chabwera, PhD,** who specializes in postcolonial literature (especially new writing) and black women writers and is the author of *Writing Black Womanhood: Feminist Writing by Four Contemporary African and Black Diaspora Women Writers*. The colleagues share a moment at the 2017 ALA Conference banquet at Yale University. These two authors also participated in a roundtable discussion with MJ "On Becoming a Successful Independent Book Author & Publisher" at the 2019 ALA Conference in Columbus, Ohio.

➤ Offer to Review Other Authors' Works.

Another way that aspiring authors get noticed is to ask someone knowledgeable about the book's subject matter or a noted author to write a foreword to their book. Some time ago, a longtime acquaintance wrote a memoir about how she survived breast cancer. Her story is uplifting. With each page, one becomes more and more intrigued with what happens next. The author, Felecia Todeh Wesley, carefully weaves in bits and pieces about her life growing up in Liberia, her immigration to America, her children, her spouse, her friends, and her employment up to the point that she first learns she has breast cancer. The manuscript reads like a mystery novel, with all its ups and downs and twists and turns. The author's storytelling skills come through like beams of light, bursts of thunder, and joy and praise. My initial role was as a beta reader, but the author eventually asked me to write the foreword to her book. I am honored to have written the foreword to Wesley's *Can't Complain: God Is Good to Me – My Story* (2020).

A Word about Book Reviews

There are four basic types of book reviews.

Manuscript Reviews, sometimes called endorsements, are done by recognized names in the genre of your book. Reviewers assess the writing style and the quality of an incomplete or a finished "advanced reader copy" (ARC). Beta readers point out areas that might need revising ahead of submission to external review. Meanwhile, if the author receives positive and robust endorsements about her book, put them on the cover design.

Imagine my surprise when an Amazon influencer requested an ARC of the published version of one of my books. Recall one of my rules, "Never give up, and keep right on writing." One never knows when someone "influential" will notice her work. But when a book reviewer from inside the publishing industry notices your work, rest assured you are doing something right. So, stay the course. And although the Amazon influencer's review does not coincide with this handbook's publication, I look forward to whatever his assessment reveals. More plainly put, whether a positive, negative, or modest review, in this business, "Ink about a book is still ink!"

Editorial Reviews, sometimes referred to as *Trade Reviews*, from bloggers and book editors associated with radio and television stations or reputable print media, such as the *New York Times*, can be priceless *if* the reviews are favorable. It is left to the author to determine whether the demographics of the respective reviewer fit her target audience—that is, the readers who are likely to buy her book(s). Unfortunately, though, some trade reviews often come at a relatively high financial cost. Highly regarded are *Publishers Weekly, Kirkus Reviews*, and *Blue Ink Review*.

Peer Reviews are revered in technical, scientific, and academic circles. During my tenure as a political science professor, I would attend conferences and listen to papers being read by my colleagues. Peer reviews typically provide constructive criticism. But they can be brutal slap-downs—rarely, if ever, neutral—as scholars and scientists, editors of journals and periodicals, practitioners of academic fields of study, scientific and technical research, and technology perform these reviews.

Consumer or *Reader Reviews* are performed by individuals who have purchased and read an author's book(s). The more "likes" amassed online—such as Amazon, Facebook, or Goodreads—the better! For those affiliated with the NCWN, our Metro-North regional rep posts his reviews on his website, www.hiddentreasurenovels.com/, as do colleagues in the other conferences in which I hold membership.

The following are excerpts from some consumer, editorial, manuscript, and reader reviews of "the Priscilla Series" that I compiled over recent years:

Priscilla Engaging in the Game of Politics

"Trilogy begins. M.J. Simms-Maddox's *Priscilla* dives into politics."
SALISBURY POST

"The author knows the inner workings of state politics, the wily maneuvers, the party bartering, and the importance of rank, experience, and sponsorship. Priscilla survives an affair with her boss, weathering it like a veteran from New York tabloid wars while writing a letter about her former allies that would have destroyed someone else in real life. It makes for good reading that keeps the reader interested." AFRICAN AMERICAN LITERATURE BOOKCLUB

"A classic bildungsroman. Simms-Maddox demonstrates her knowledge of the game firsthand with great descriptive details and political jargon throughout this thriller." MARIE LINTON UMEH, Ph.D.

"'When writing a novel, a writer should create living people, people, not characters. A character is a caricature,' said Ernest Hemingway. And a living person is precisely what Simms-Maddox has created in her book." OSIRIS VALLEJO

"I have read many books, both fiction and nonfiction, and all of the authors have had more experience than [Simms-Maddox]. Yet [her] novel eclipses them all. Being [her] first novel, Priscilla demonstrates vocabulary that mesmerizes the reader; I was drawn into the story and couldn't put the book down. I confess, the graphic description of a daughter seeing her father's illness and death, tears welled up in my eyes. [She has] the gift of a seasoned writer." RETIRED POSTAL WORKER, East Orange, New Jersey

Mystery in Harare: Priscilla's Journey into Southern Africa

"M.J. Simms-Maddox is an excellent writer. There is a Maqoma in [her]."
THEMBA NGABA, Amava Heritage Publishing, Ltd., South Africa

5 Stars!
★ ★ ★ ★ ★
BEST BOOK
Chanticleer
Book Reviews

CIBA 2019 M&M AWARDED REVIEW of:
Mystery In Harare: Priscilla's Journey into Southern Africa
Genre(s): Historical African Fiction, Terrorism Thrillers,
Travel Adventure Fiction
Rating: 5 Stars; Highly recommended
Reviewer: Lily Amanda

In M.J. Simms-Maddox's atmospheric thriller, *Mystery in Harare: Priscilla's Journey into Southern Africa*, a former legislative aide's wedding day turns deadly.

Before she can even take her vows, her soon-to-be husband is murdered in cold blood in front of her and those in attendance. Priscilla catches a glimpse of the murderer before succumbing to unconsciousness. She's been drugged, and the kidnappers will confound and surprise readers.

When Priscilla gains consciousness, she is no longer in the United States but in the hinterland of Zimbabwe, Africa.

Mystery In Harare is undoubtedly a successful terrorism thriller novel and a good place to start understanding the underbelly of the period of Apartheid in South Africa and its implications on all of its citizenry.

Mystery in Harare: Priscilla's Journey into Southern Africa by M.J. Simms-Maddox won First Place in the CIBAs 2019 Mystery and Mayhem Book Awards and comes highly recommended.

Three Metal Pellets

COMMENTS FROM BOOK CLUB MEMBERS at the 2019 National Black Book Festival, Houston, Texas, include:

> "Refreshing to meet an author of a series about a contemporary African American woman comparable to Walter Mosley's Easy Rawlins and Leonid McGill."

> "Finally, a Black female protagonist who is not a former slave, maid, prostitute ...."

> "The intimidating [book] cover is captivating."

"Timely. The author takes us by the hand and leads us into a world about the election of America's first Black president, whose background competes with the likes of the Rockefellers and the Vanderbilts. A fifth-generation Barbadian American, Fleetwood Marshall Hollingsworth engages the only remaining quest to establish his family's legacy, the American presidency! Remember, after all, this is a novel, and you may have to keep telling yourself that because it seems so real." MICHAEL D. CONNOR, Actor, Playwright, and Theatrical Director

Whose Writing Style Does Yours Match?

According to a *ScoreIt*[TM] analysis of *Special Envoy*, "M.J. Simms-Maddox's writing style most closely matches the writing styles of Tom Clancy's *Locked On* and *Command Authority* and John Connolly's *Empire*."

The genre is integral. *Special Envoy* is adult fiction: thriller-suspense-action-adventure-terrorism-espionage.

ScoreIt[TM] software analyzes an author's writing style and correlates it against similar styles among other authors along four dimensions: authorial vocabulary, expressive complexity, grammar, and tonal quality. See the results below for the top three authors with whom Simms-Maddox's writing style matches most closely for this novel:

ScoreIt[TM] **Analysis of** *Special Envoy*

Title and Genre	Authorial Vocabulary	Expressive Complexity	Grammar	Tonal Quality
Locked On Adult Fiction/ Thriller	99%	93%	99%	86%
Empire Adult Fiction/ Science Fiction	96%	95%	77%	99%
Command Authority Adult Fiction/ Thriller	98%	84%	99%	84%

Independent evaluations of an author's writing style of this order are priceless. Insert this type of information on your book covers.

Also, *NetGalley*, which also comes at a cost, ".... connects reviewers with authors... and gets your latest release in front of the reader community." For more about *NetGalley* and other reviewers, consult Nettles' *Business Essentials for Writers: How to Make Money in an Every-Changing Industry* (2019, 98) in the section on "Marketing Plan."

Step Seven:
Now, Create Your Own Roadmap.

To reiterate: there is no foolproof way—or any precise method—to write a book and ultimately publish it. But there are industry standards that all successful authors typically follow, one way or another. Remember: what might seem simple in this step-by-step approach has taken me years to learn. And I am still learning.

Regardless, only after performing the steps outlined in this handbook can you learn what works best for you—hence, this final step.

Suppose you prefer not to obtain the publishing essentials in Step Four and to convert your MS Word manuscript into book format, digital, e-book, and audiobook versions in Step Five. In that case, I strongly recommend that you retain the services of a professional. Perhaps one of the hybrids or other publishing industry specialists listed in the "Trending in Hybrid and Indie Book Publishing" section best suits your needs. Or you might prefer to persevere in your search for a literary agent.

But if you are technology-proficient and can master the conversion processes, "Hooray!" As for me, I dread doing the conversions, but when I see the notice, "Files meet the international standards," I then have affirmed myself for myself, and that is a good feeling.

I encourage you to continue leafing through these pages and modifying them for what works best for you. Then, as you become a successful indie author-publisher, pen your own journey, and help someone else along the way.

Last, I have a selfish reason for encouraging aspiring authors to become indies. As a semi-retired college professor, I find it exhilarating to hear former students singing my praises. But if just one writer follows these guidelines and publishes her first or next book, I will have succeeded in bringing someone else along the way.

Blessings.

Appendix A

A Description and an Example of a Manuscript Cover Page

Appendix

As a rule, always adhere to the guidelines for manuscript submissions. Some literary agents, acquisition editors, and publishers prefer that an author's *first* manuscript be limited to 100,000 words or fewer, but I write lengthier novels. So, my editors have come to accept that my work almost always exceeds the norm.

Below is an excerpt from my manuscript for *Three Metal Pellets*. I used Courier merely to illustrate the font to younger writers and other writers who might be unfamiliar with it. However, the sample does not allow you to see the margins on an 8.5" x 11" sheet of white paper.

Pay particular attention to the information typically required for manuscript submissions for the first (cover) page.

- ✓ Place the author's contact information in the top flush left-hand corner. You, the contact person, are the one to whom the publisher compensates for the work.
    - o Although professional memberships are optional, list only your memberships related to writing.
    - o Do *not* divulge your social security number.

- ✓ Center your book's title and byline approximately one-half of the way down the first page. The byline is your name or your *pseudonym* (the person who receives credit for the story—that is, the person in whose name the book will be published).

- ✓ The standard indentation for paragraphs is one-half inch, .5". As noted earlier, I do not indent the first paragraph of any section, scene, or chapter in my books. Instead, my first paragraph is flush left, after which I indent all subsequent paragraphs at .3" or .4". But if you are a new writer, use the standard one-half-inch indentation from the beginning to the end of your manuscript.

Appendix

M. J. Simms-Maddox, Ph.D.
Mailing Address
Telephone
Email

Membership: North Carolina Writers' Network

Word Count 173,000

THREE METAL PELLETS

M. J. Simms-Maddox, Ph.D.

1

The Invitation and Chapungu Sculpture Park

It was time for Priscilla to become the woman she was meant
to be.

Only a month after Priscilla returned to Columbus from
the press conference in West Germany, she found that the
services of her home-based business, P. J. Austin and
Associates, Incorporated, were suddenly in high demand. But
she was not interested in any of the requests. She had
assumed, correctly, that most of the prospective clients had

only wanted to play off her notoriety. And even before her time in Africa, around the time of the Ohio premiere of the documentary *Mandela*, she had begun conducting business that carried substance, business that was "earthy," not superficial. So, in her upscale West Third Street PR home-office in Victorian Village, she waited and waited and waited for something "earthy" to come across her desk.

****

Appendix B

An Example of a Query Letter

Appendix

Date

Literary Agent's Name and Title
Agency
Address
City, State zip code

Hello (first name, or Ms., Mr., or the Title and the agent's last name):

Mystery in Harare: Priscilla's Journey into Southern Africa chronicles the coming-of-age and the adventures of a carefree and enterprising young woman abducted from her "comfort level" in the American Midwest to the savannas of southern Africa—early post-apartheid-ruled Zimbabwe and South Africa.

> The bride pauses for an instant before walking down the aisle to marry a man she likes but does not love, and in that hesitant moment, a shot rings out, and then another. The groom falls. Blood stains the sanctuary.

> Priscilla J. "PJ" Austin, a magnetic, up–and–coming, African American baby boomer, catches a glimpse of the shooter before everything goes black for the bride...

Mystery in Harare is a stylish, fast-paced, character-driven thriller that unravels the secrets behind this carnage at a Midwestern American Black church.

The novel uses race, feminism, history, politics, and the cozy milieu of an upscale 1980s African American family to portray the coming-of-age of a carefree and enterprising young woman who believes—as her minister-father has told her—she can do anything.

But Priscilla's fortitude is sorely tried as she awakens, sometime later—sedated and confused, on the outskirts of Harare, Zimbabwe—to face the adventure of her life. Along the way, there is mayhem, murder, mistaken identities, and a barbed reunion with Carlton Bernhardt—a swarthy, intrepid special operative who may be her one true love.

Mystery in Harare appeals to the adult women's commercial fiction market and the subgenres of ethnic, multicultural, and African American readers. Its primary appeal is women 20 and older, but it also reaches Young Adult female readers. By genre, *Mystery in Harare* is a thriller. Priscilla is a modern heroine who happens to be Black, but the novel has a broad appeal that transcends race. Of particular interest to readers is its tender depiction of a middle-class African American

Appendix

family whose struggles with contemporary prejudice illuminate the universal human condition.

Published by M. J. Simms-Maddox, Inc. in August 2017, *Mystery in Harare—Priscilla's Journey into Southern Africa* is approximately 120,000 words.

The author chairs the Department of History & Political Science at Livingstone College in Salisbury, NC. She earned her Ph.D. in political science from The Ohio State University, has served as a legislative aide in the Ohio Senate, has operated her own public relations agency, and has published in various academic, community, and religious publications. She is affiliated with the African Literature Association, the North Carolina Writers' Network, and the Women's National Book Association. Her first major literary work is the Priscilla trilogy.

Thank you for taking the time to read my query letter.

Respectfully,

M. J. Simms-Maddox, Author

Appendix C

An Example of Front Matter

Three Metal Pellets

ALSO BY M. J. SIMMS-MADDOX

PRISCILLA Engaging in the Game of Politics

MYSTERY IN HARARE

Three Metal Pellets

M. J. SIMMS-MADDOX, Ph.D.

M. J. Simms-Maddox, Inc. ~ Salisbury, NC

Appendix

Three Metal Pellets

Published by
M. J. Simms-Maddox, Inc. ~ Salisbury, NC
https://www.mjsimmsmaddoxinc.com (https://www.novelsbymj.com)

ISBN: 978-1-7322406-1-2

Jacket Cover by JustJina.US
Logo Design by John Simms
Webmaster JustJina.US
Author's Photo by John Daniels of Salisbury, NC

Dedication

To the loving memory of my nephew, Germane Kevin Harris, who was murdered on June 6, 2008, in San Francisco, and to my sister—Paulette, his mother—may she find peace.

Appendix

[This page is intentionally blank]

Appendix

ACKNOWLEDGMENTS

Thanks to two of my colleagues and friends, Michael D. Connor and Terri Porter, for encouraging me to create a story about the first African American president, and although the election of the first African American to the U. S. presidency occurred with Barack Obama in 2008, this story was situated twenty years earlier in 1988.

Any misstatements about the American presidential election campaign process are entirely mine.

I am forever grateful to my mom, Hazel B. Owens Simms—"my sweet inspiration" and our family's first published author, to my trusted editor, Lee Titus Elliott—who I tend to go after and mess up his excellent editing, to Linda Ellis Eastman—for setting me on the path to publishing the Priscilla trilogy, and to my darling husband Odinga—for his moral support and unwavering consideration for our loss of quality time together.

My goal in this endeavor was to bring the adventures of Priscilla J. (PJ) Austin to a conclusion, but that did not happen.

There was no intention by me to cast aspersions on anyone remotely similar to or in any way related to the characters or the events portrayed throughout this work of fiction.

All too often, novices like me are dissuaded from following our dreams. But from the start, many of you put your money on the table and bought my books, and then you shared them with others. I am so very grateful for your kindness and belief in me, all of which have fueled my confidence to keep right on writing.

Appendix

[This page is intentionally blank]

Appendix

Contents

Appendix

Appendix D

An Example of a Front Book Cover

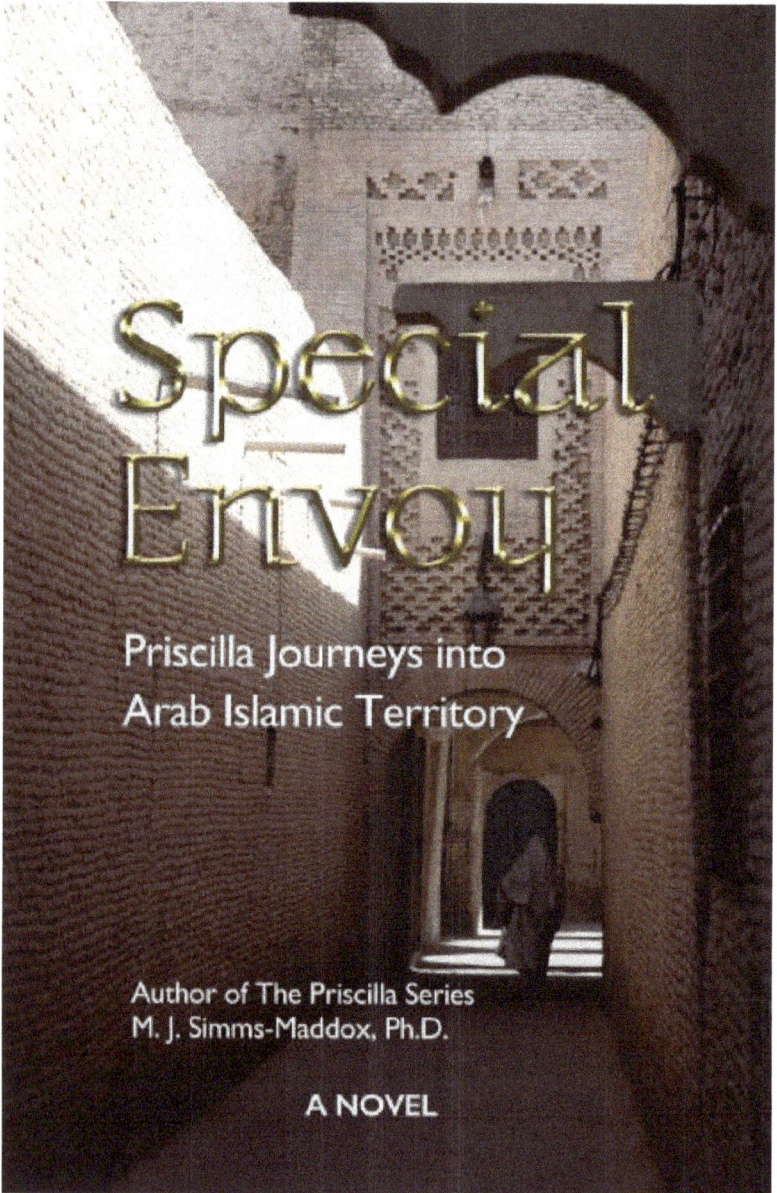

Special
Envoy

Priscilla Journeys into
Arab Islamic Territory

Author of The Priscilla Series
M. J. Simms-Maddox, Ph.D.

A NOVEL

Appendix E

An Example of Text and a Price Barcode on a Back Book Cover

Appendix

In *Special Envoy*, the fourth installment in what has become "The Priscilla Series," political science professor-turned-fiction writer M. J. Simms-Maddox, Ph.D., creates more adventure and intrigue for Priscilla.

Unfortunately, CF Captain Smirnoff and the two CF soldiers who accompanied him did not see the floor of the bin as it lowered. Before the transfer truck—which was believed to be carrying the limousine in which Priscilla's entourage rode—had pulled out of the parking lot, the other man who accompanied the chauffeur had gotten out of the limo—out of the view of the CF captain and his two CF soldiers—and pressed a lever on the wall inside the huge bin. The limousine lowered two stories through a false bottom, down into the Earth. So the CF captain and his two CF soldiers had not witnessed that scene.

As the slow thump-like movement of the luxury limo lowered into the depths of the Earth, Priscilla's claustrophobia and vertigo surfaced. It first began when the limo rode onto the ramp inside the closely contained bin. Her heart beat faster. Beads of sweat formed on her forehead. She experienced difficulty breathing. Priscilla panicked and squirmed in her seat. There was nothing that anybody could do to help her. Her meclizine was in her luggage, back at the Rainbow Towers Hotel and Conference Center in Harare.

Then, as Harry attempted to transmit another message to his superior officer about the latest episode in their precarious predicament, he lost service on his old-style cell phone.

So, apart from Priscilla, Melanie, and Harry, no one else knew that they were inside a limousine, two levels down deep in the Earth, in the parking lot of a technology company in Amman.

$49.99

ISBN 978-1-7322406-0-5

54999>

9 781732 240605

Appendix F

The Making of the Priscilla Series

Appendix

The Making of the Priscilla Series

Not all of us grow up yearning to become authors; for some of us, becoming an author just happens. My first major attempt at writing was to compose an autobiographical piece—to recapture my family history or roots. But one thing led to another, and before I knew it, I was changing the names of people and places and embellishing events and incidents.

At the time, in the late 1990s, I knew little about the publishing industry. I sent an unsolicited voluminous manuscript to a publisher in Berkeley, California. The publisher wrote me a kind rejection letter complimenting my style of writing. But he also gave me the name and contact information for an editor and ended his correspondence with, "You have three books in one." Thus began my journey as a writer of fiction.

A lesson learned the hard way. After an incredibly long relationship with that Berkeley editor—who critiqued my work but did not edit it—our relationship ceased. Critiquing is different from editing. Avoid editors who only critique. You want someone who will help you improve your writing, not merely critique it.

Here I pause to encourage all authors to learn how to describe their work in concise terms; a description often referred to as *"an elevator pitch,"* "a Twitter pitch," or "a Pixar pitch" (a brief presentation of the narrative). Be prepared when someone says, "Tell me about your book." All right, so that is easier said than done. It took me nearly a decade to come up with the following pitch about my books, and it still needs refining:

> The Priscilla Series chronicles the coming-of-age and the
> adventures of an African American young woman (Priscilla is
> her name) abducted from her comfort level in the American
> Midwest to the savannas and the wilds of Southern Africa—in
> early post-apartheid Zimbabwe and South Africa—where, even
> more unexpectedly, she finds herself on the run. But Priscilla
> eventually returns home where, finally, she becomes the woman
> she was meant to be.

Appendix

The Priscilla series began with a recurring dream about a conversation that I had had with my father, a great storyteller. It had not been a bad discussion; instead, it had been one in which a loving father shares precious thoughts about his love and hopes for his beloved daughter. I told a friend (Ada White Taylor) about that dream, and she said, "MJ, the next time you have that dream, write it down." As I began penning that dream, I found myself reflecting that I had served as a legislative aide in the Ohio Senate in the early 1980s. Thus started the Priscilla trilogy. My point is that the dream was merely the *catalyst for writing*—not necessarily what I should write about. But whatever it is—write it down.

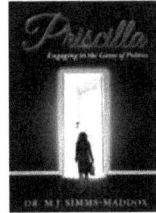

It took me almost one year to extract my first book from those "three books in one" mentioned earlier. Then, I spent a decade receiving "critiques" from the Berkeley editor. All right, so I was slow on the uptake.

Of the three other editors that I had researched, interviewed, and ended up retaining, one of them was excellent at substantial copyediting. His name is Lee Titus Elliott. Lee also helps with restructuring. The second editor, Laurie Devine, is excellent at developmental editing, and she has enlightened me about "significant" name changes, not to mention tweaking character development. It has been my experience that it sometimes takes more than one editor to work on a book, especially the lengthy ones I write.

The third editor—based in Britain and who, I later learned, was a renowned author—recommended that I work with the two American editors because, at the time, the pound sterling was valued at twice the American dollar. But it was the British editor, Alice McVeigh, who also enlightened me about the significance of my work—that American literature is virtually void of stories about contemporary professional African American women [more specifically, Black women with agency] and that books like mine have much potential.

In my search for *a literary agent*, I must have written hundreds—well, maybe not hundreds—but many query letters to literary agents for almost three years. Then, in the fall of 2015, my sister-in-law, Clintina Cooper Simms, suggested that I contact Linda Ellis Eastman of the Professional Woman Network (PWN). I did not know that Linda was an accomplished author and a seasoned editor. Nor was I aware of her connections to the publishing industry.

Appendix

Linda performed the final editing of my first novel, *Priscilla Engaging in the Game of Politics*. She then turned the manuscript over to her team—Professional Woman Publishing, LLC—who designed the cover, converted the document into digital printing format, published the book in my name, and then turned the finished product—and all publishing rights—back over to me. (By the way, I would categorize the PWP, LLC as a hybrid publisher.) That marked the beginning of my desire to publish my work myself.

My second novel stems from a series of travel stories. For several years, my family, mainly my mother and I, would pick a place to visit. Before I wrote my second novel, we had toured the West Indies, Britain, France, Italy, Greece, Zimbabwe, Ghana, Senegal, and many other places, all of which I chronicled in a journal. So, I set about writing a series of travel stories, or so I thought.

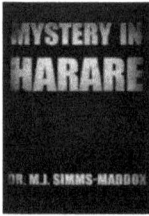

But the more I edited the travel stories, the flatter they fell. Frustrated, I told another friend, Michael D. Connor, about my situation. He suggested that I resume writing about Priscilla and that I give her "something juicy!" Yes, he used the word "juicy." Then, before I knew it, I wrote a love scene between Priscilla and the man with whom she once shared a passionate love affair.

A short time later, for some reason unknown to me, I began wondering about what had happened on the world stage back in the middle 1980s. Terrorism! Airports and densely populated cities around the globe were bombed and otherwise devastated. I remembered that I had taken a trip to visit one of my sisters and her family, who resided near an air force base outside Croton in the United Kingdom. When I arrived at the Heathrow Airport, crowds of family and friends anxiously awaited their loved ones. That was when I learned about some Islamic militants who had hijacked a TWA passenger jetliner en route from Athens to Rome. At the time, I, like many Americans, did not give much thought to terrorism because we viewed that as "something that happens elsewhere." Eventually, though, I researched other terrorist activities that occurred during that time. The CIA website was useful.

I also drew upon my experiences during a six-week visit to Zimbabwe. The tourist sites, the magnificent landscapes, and the safaris all play prominently in the story.

Appendix

As a political scientist, I already knew about the cultures and politics of Zimbabwe and South Africa, particularly the apartheid system, and I was also familiar with the mineral-rich territory of the southern part of the African continent. So I created a conglomerate of mine owners and distributors of diamonds, gold, and platinum that were, of course, pro-Nationalists. I named the conglomerate "Executive Committee of the South African Nationalists Movement" (the SANM). Then I created an enforcement arm and called it "Patrol Guard" (the PG). Why did I make up a terrorist organization that was based in South Africa?

For one thing, the world's eyes were on the growing terrorist activities of people from the Middle East. And even though the situations in the Middle East were devastating and remain so today, there was comparatively little attention given to the plight of the Black people in Zimbabwe and South Africa—hence my focus on those two nations. Sure, news stories covered those two countries, particularly the corrupt regime of Robert Mugabe and the blazing apartheid regime in South Africa, not to mention Nelson Mandela's imprisonment. Still, it seemed to me that there was much benign neglect of the plight of the Black people—the majority population—in those two countries.

My creative "juices" flowed. The next thing I knew, I was putting Priscilla in the throes of terrorist activity, but not on American soil or in Europe, for that matter. Instead, I chose Zimbabwe and South Africa. The book's title reflects that much of what happens to Priscilla occurs in Harare. So the material in those travel stories came in handy, after all.

When my editors read the manuscript for *Mystery in Harare: Priscilla's Journey into Southern Africa*, they both got back to me immediately and said that I had written a thriller and that it was a darn good one, too.

Once again, I benefited from the services of Linda Ellis Eastman of the PWN and its publishing branch. They published *Mystery in Harare* in my name and turned the final product—and all the publishing rights—back over to me, as well.

Appendix

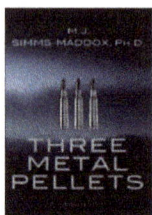

I spent an equal amount of time writing *Three Metal Pellets* as it had taken me to pen *Mystery in Harare*—six months. Writing comes easily when a writer is onto a good story and in a suitable writing mood. This novel came about after talking to fans, friends, and colleagues about the presidency of Barack Obama. But there already existed a wealth of information about President Obama, who, by the way, is a real person. Besides, I wanted to write a *novel* about the first president who happens to be African (Black) American. So that was what I did.

From the start, however, I kept asking myself why there were still people in the world, especially here in the United States, who held ridiculous stereotypes about Black people. In the United States, we have people of all lifestyles and socioeconomic stations—even billionaires. So, I began the novel by creating a presidential hopeful from a prominent and wealthy family like the Kennedys, the Rockefellers, the Roosevelts, and the Vanderbilts. But the size of the wealth was not my focal point. Instead, I focused on the fictitious family's quest to build its legacy—a universal concept that anybody of any race, ethnic group, or social station can relate to. Ah, heck, it's "the American Dream."

By this point, I had come upon the third book's publication in what eventually became the Priscilla trilogy. Priscilla is well-known by fans as a public relations consultant. So, I open the story after she returns from her first time in southern Africa, in her home-office, where she waits and waits for something of substance to come across her desk. Around one year later, in 1987, she receives a handwritten request to spearhead marketing a relatively unknown presidential hopeful. The story takes off from there.

The political scientist in me threaded a presidential election campaign throughout the plot—another example of writing about what you know. I created a story from the exploratory phase of a presidential campaign to the Iowa caucuses and the New Hampshire primaries through the national political party convention and the General Election. Throughout, I show how the presidential election campaign team constantly challenges Priscilla. Like it was when she was regarded as an outsider in the Ohio Senate in the first novel, she must prove herself all along the way.

Priscilla's secret lover and his eccentric family play prominently in the story. I also write more, but I do not wish to give away the plot.

172

Appendix

Sometime later, I realized that the book's title needed a subtitle, which I have yet to attach.

Unlike my first two books, I published *Three Metal Pellets* entirely myself. My earlier experiences with the PWN team had prepared me for that moment. So I went for it, and I have been going for it ever since.

Shown from left to right are former colleagues of the author from Livingstone College: Professors Osiris Vallejo, Michael D. Connor, Christopher White, and P. Jane Splawn. (The woman in the middle is unnamed.) The scene is the launch for *Special Envoy*, Jan. 20, 2020, in the Hilliard Room, Livingstone College campus.

Special Envoy: Priscilla Journeys into Arab Islamic Territory is an example of how, when an author thinks she has exhausted all that she can do with a character, more comes to mind. When I had completed the trilogy, I just knew that I had finished writing about Priscilla. But I had another idea.

It is the turn of 1990, and most Americans are still relatively oblivious to terrorism. Most are unaware of happenings behind-the-scenes and off-camera with the brave men and women in the diplomatic corps and intelligence gathering communities whose job is to generate peace among nations.

Appendix

Therefore, I use Priscilla to illustrate some of what happens behind the scenes. If you have read the second book of the series, some intelligence officers approach Priscilla about entering their realm at the end of *Mystery in Harare*. But it is not until this fourth novel that I portray her as an intelligence agent. This book involved lots of research and took me about one year to compose.

Since much of the narrative deals with Arab Islamic cultures, I called upon my political scientist instincts to craft plots about American foreign policy with Middle Eastern nations in such ways as not to put anyone to sleep.

Approaching retirement and with the pendulum of my life moving from side to side too rapidly, I determined that I wanted at least one classic to my credit before my demise. I published *Special Envoy* in classic form: hardcover, dust jacket, Smyth-sewn, crème-color paper stock, and the like ($49.00 ©2019) and available only on my website or wherever I exhibit my books.

I also published a case-bound version entitled *Special Envoy 1* ($34.99 ©2020), available at the usual online sites, IngramSpark, my website, and a bookstore near you. (I revised the title to *Special Envoy 1* because, as it turns out, this is the first of at least one more novel portraying Priscilla as a special envoy.)

Then, almost immediately, I was inspired to write a story portraying Priscilla without any terrorist activity. I wanted to show more of her personal life and her romantic side. For whatever reason, I thought about a plot involving art, notably the Metropolitan Museum of Art—hence, *The Mysterious Affair at the Met* (2021). Although the Met board of trustees retains Priscilla for her public relations expertise, they have no way of knowing that she will use her skills as an intelligence agent to avert some of the deceit, fraud, and skullduggery that could quickly become the scandal of the decade, if not the century.

The subtitle is "Priscilla Plays in High Cotton in the World of Highly-Valued Works of Art." Most publishers do not like titles longer than five words. For sure, a subtitle as lengthy as this one would be unacceptable. Just think. You can create your own rules by publishing your work yourself—another reason I publish my work myself.

Appendix

Another lesson learned: while publishing *The Mysterious Affair at the Met*, I produced *Creative Writing – the Basics* and *Self-Publishing Your Way*, taking away much-needed attention from finishing the novel. Meanwhile, shortly after enabling the distribution of the novel, I noticed some problems with its content. Therefore, I halted its distribution and waited until I finished producing these two handbooks before revising *The Mysterious Affair at the Met*. I learned to work on one major project at a time.

Meanwhile, and much to my surprise, I received an offer from a hybrid publisher to publish *The Mysterious Affair at the Met*. But that offer would not have come had I not published the book in the first place. So, another edition will be published and, in all formats, i.e., hardcover, paperback, e-book, and audiobook, between 2022 and 2023.

There you have it, and there is more to come in the Priscilla Series—who would have thought!

Appendix G

An Example of an Online Permission Request Form

Appendix

FOR ILLUSTRATION ONLY

PUBLISHER
(Sample) Permission Request Form

Publishers generally indicate turnaround time to obtain permission rights at the beginning of the form, such as "Allow six weeks for a response." Take notice of the response time, particularly if your publication date conflicts with it. You may have to change the publication date on your distributor's website. Avoid publishing a book requiring permission rights ahead of obtaining permission.

One of the first items the publisher asks is the name or the title of the work or which you seek permission rights. See the following example:

Title: (Insert the title that you want permission to use the copyrighted material, for example, *Their Eyes Were Watching God.*)

Some publishers ask for the genre, such as fiction or non-fiction and so forth.

Since popular books have been published often and sometimes by different imprints (publishers), most publishers ask for the publication date of the title you are using and its ISBN. For *Their Eyes Were Watching God*, it is as follows: © 1990, ISBN: 0-06-092141-8.

Exact content, such as the page count (the number of pages, if applicable, that you want to use from *Their Eyes Were Watching God*). Or if sentences, paragraphs, or particular sections, indicate in precise terms. See the example below:

> "Here, finally, was a woman" through "they had ever encountered in literature" on p. xi and from "Ships at a distance have every man's wish on board" through "Pheoby stood up sharply" on pp. 1-3.

Three pages.

Appendix

Publishers also ask <u>where the copyrighted material will appear and in what format(s)</u>. In the case of this handbook, I provided the following information:

A HANDBOOK for Emerging and Seasoned Authors: An Insider's Step-by-Step Approach to Becoming a Successful Indie Book Author and Publisher *

M. J. Simms-Maddox, Author/Publisher   Lee Titus Elliott, Editor
mjsimmsmaddox@gmail.com   (Sometimes, I list my name
as the editor if I paraphrase the copyrighted material.)

Tentative Publication Date: March 15, 2021

Planned Formats: hardcover case bound

Print Runs: 1,000

I also provided the pages from my manuscript to illustrate how and where the copyrighted material from *Their Eyes Were Watching God* would be used.

I provided my email address because the publisher asked for it on the form.

Do not be surprised if the publisher notes, "Additional permission is required from another source for world rights." (In this particular case, recall that I needed to obtain permission rights from the British publisher to sell this handbook in the United Kingdom and the British Commonwealth, which I eventually secured.)

Publishers might also ask authors about the nature of use, such as electronic rights and languages, for all editions and media. (Be prepared to answer those questions as well.)

Note: the exact content of permission request forms, fees, and the turnaround times depend on the title's publisher.

*The original title of this handbook changed to *Creative Writing and Self-Publishing Your Way*.

A Checklist of Publishing Essentials

Action Steps	In Progress	Date Completed
Create Your Writing Régime		
Establish a Budget		
Acquire the Proper Tools		
Write Your Manuscript		
Retain an Editor		
Write a Query Letter (If applicable)		
Land a Literary Agent (If applicable)		
Retain an Accountant		
Retain an Attorney		
Get a Headshot		
Create a Professional Name or Pseudonym (If applicable)		
Obtain an EIN		
Incorporate		
Open a Business Bank Account		
Obtain Permission Rights (If applicable)		
Copyright Manuscript		
Apply for a PCN		
Write Your Biography		
Write a Blurb or Hook about Book		
Write a Synopsis of Your Book		
Purchase ISBN(s)		
Purchase Price Barcode(s)		
Develop and Upload the Metadata		
Choose Distributor(s)		
Choose an On-Demand (Digital) Printer (If applicable)		
Choose an Offset Printer (If applicable)		

A Checklist of Publishing Essentials

Retain a Web Administrator (If applicable)
    a.   Purchase a Platform
    b.   Build a Website
    c. Create a Domain Name		

Purchase a Card Reader		
Convert an MS Word Manuscript into a book format *or* Hire a Hybrid Publisher		
Convert an MS Word-formatted document into an ISO-Validated Digital File *or* Hire a Hybrid Publisher		
Produce an E-Book *or* Hire a Hybrid Publisher		
Produce an Audiobook *or* Hire a Professional Narrator from one of the Audiobook Production Houses		

Promote Your Book(s):
    a.   Schedule Promotions and Exhibitions, Travel, and Share News about Your Book
    b.   Enter Book Contests
    c.   Join Professional Associations
    d.   Review Other Authors' Work
    e. Solicit Book Reviews		

Create Your Own Roadmap.		
List Other Things You Need to Do or Desire as an Author:		

References

Adichie, Chimamanda Ngozi. AMERICANAH. New York: Anchor Books,
     A Division of Random House LLC, 2013.

Aidoo, Ama Ata. *Changes: A Love Story*. New York: The Feminist Press at
     The City University of New York, 1993.

Boyce Davies, Carole. *Black Women Writing and Identity: Migrations of subject*.
     New York: Routledge Taylor & Francis Group, 1994. (Credit: Page 33,
     Copyright 1994 from *Black Women Writing and Identity: Migrations of*
     subject by Carole Boyce Davies. Reproduced by permission of Taylor and
     Francis Group, LLC, a division of Informa plc.)

Chabwera, Elinettie. *Writing Black Womanhood: Feminist Writing By Four*
     Contemporary African and Black Diaspora Women Writers: Saarbrücken,
     Deutschland: LAP Lambert Academic Publishing GmbH & Co. KG,
     2010, p.1.

Dangarembga, Tsitsi. *Nervous Conditions*. New York: McDougal Littell, a
     division of Houghton Mifflin Company, 1997.

DeMille, Nelson. *Up Country*. New York: Warner Books, Inc., 2002.

Ellison, Ralph. *Invisible Man*. New York: Vintage International Edition,
     Random House, Inc., Oct. 1990.

Emenyonu, Ernest N., Editor. *New Women's Writing in* AFRICAN LITERATURE,
     African Literature Today, Vol. 24. Oxford: James Currey and Trenton,
     New Jersey: Africa World Press, 2004.

Guide to Literary Agents 2020. New York: Writer's Digest Books – Penguin
     Random House, LLC, 2019.

Head, Bessie. *When Rain Clouds Gather*. New York: Simon and Schuster, 1968.

_____. *Maru*. New York: The McCall Publishing Company, 1971.

_____. *A Question of Power*. London: Heinemann, 1974.

Hurston, Zora Neale. *Their Eyes Were Watching God*. New York: Harper
     Perennial, a division of HarperCollins Publishers, Inc., 1990.
     (Credits: ... Pages 1-3 from *Their Eyes Were Watching God* by Zora
     Neale Hurston. Copyright (c) 1937 by Zora Neale Hurston. Renewed
     (c)1965 by John C. Hurston and Joel Hurston. Used by permission of
     HarperCollins Publishers *and* Little, Brown Book Group Limited.)

References

Hynes, Professor James. *Writing Fiction: Storytelling Tips & Techniques*. Chantilly, Virginia: The Teaching Company, LLC, The Great Courses, (P)2014.

La Plante, Alice. *Method and Madness: The Making of a Story: A Guide to Writing Fiction*. New York: W. W. Norton & Company, 2008.

Marshall, Carmen Rose. *Black Professional Women in Recent American Fiction*. Jefferson, North Carolina: McFarland & Co., Inc., 2004. (The use of material from pages 151-162, 165-166, and 170 in *Black Professional Women in Recent American Fiction* © 2004 Carmen Rose Marshall was used by permission of McFarland & Company, Inc., Box 611, Jefferson NC 28640 www.mcfarlandbooks.com.)

NDiaye, Marie. *Three Strong Women*. London: MacLehose Press, 2012.

Nettles, James P. *Business Essentials for Writers: How to Make Money in an Ever-Changing Industry*. Charlotte: Author Essentials Publications, 2019. (Permission granted by the publisher.)

Nfah-Abbenyi, Juliana Makuchi. *Gender in African Women's Writing: Identity, Sexuality, and Difference*. Bloomington and Indianapolis: Indiana University Press, 1997. (Credit: Pages 1-2 from *Gender in African women's writing: identity, sexuality, and difference* © 1997 by Juliana M. Nfah-Abbenyi by permission of Indiana University Press.)

Novel & Short Story Writer's Market, 40th Edition. New York: Writer's Digest Books – Penguin Publishing Group, 2021.

Nwapa, Flora. *Efuru*. London: Heinemann Educational Books, 1966.

_____. *Conversations*. Enugu: Tana, 1993.

_____. *The First Lady*. Enugu: Tana, 1993.

Phiri, Virginia. *Highway Queen*. Harare: Corals Services, 2010.

Rehder, Jessie. *The Young Writer at Work*, First Edition, The Odyssey Press, Inc., 1962, Seventh Printing, Indianapolis: The Bobbs-Merrill Company, Inc. 1977. (Every reasonable effort was made to obtain permission rights to use the material in Jessie Rehder's *The Young Writer at Work* © 1962 The Odyssey Press, Inc., First Edition, seventh printing, 1977, The Bobbs-Merrill Company, Inc. I am therefore using the standard scholarly form of acknowledgment, i.e., publisher, author, title, and the like.)

Reuter, Claudia. *Yes, You Can Do This! How Women Start Up, Scale Up, and Build the Life They Want*. Hoboken: John Wiley & Sons, Inc., 2020.

Shetterly, Margot Lee. *Hidden Figures: The Story of African-American Women Who Helped Win the Space War*. New York: William Morrow/HarperCollins, 2016.

References

Simms-Maddox, M. J. *Priscilla Engaging in the Game of Politics.* Salisbury, North Carolina: M. J. Simms-Maddox, Inc. in consultation with Professional Woman Publishing, LLC of Louisville, Kentucky, 2016; 2004.

_____. *Mystery in Harare: Priscilla's Journey into Southern Africa.* Salisbury, NC: M. J. Simms-Maddox, Inc. in consultation with Professional Woman Publishing, LLC of Louisville, Kentucky, 2017.

_____. *Three Metal Pellets.* (Self-published, 2018).

_____. *Special Envoy: Priscilla Journeys into Arab Islamic Territory.* (Self-published, 2019).

_____. *Special Envoy 1: Priscilla Journeys into Arab Islamic Territory,* revised edition. (Self-published, 2020).

_____. *The Mysterious Affair at the Met – Priscilla Plays in High Cotton in the World of Highly-Valued Works of Art.* (Self-published, 2021).

Sword, Helen. *Air & Light & Time & Space: How Successful Academics Write.* Cambridge, Massachusetts: Harvard University Press, 2017.

The Chicago Manual of Style – The Essential Guide for Writers, Editors, and Publishers, 17th Edition. Chicago: The University of Chicago Press, 2017.

Tolkien, J. R. R. *The Lord of the Rings - The Fellowship of the Ring.* New York: Ballantine Books, 2018; Del Rey Mass Market Edition, 2018.

Umeh, Marie Linton. *Flora Nwapa: A Pen and A Press.* New York: Transatlantic Books of NY, 2010.

Wharton, Edith. *The Writing of Fiction.* New York: Scribner, 1997.

Writer'sDigest.com

Writer's Market, 100th Edition. New York: Writer's Digest Books – Penguin Publishing Group, 2021.

Photo by Sean Meyers Photography

M. J. Simms-Maddox is an indie author and the creator and publisher of the Priscilla Series.

The South Carolina native grew up in the Snowbelt of western New York and currently resides in North Carolina. She earned her PhD in political science from The Ohio State University, has served as a legislative aide in the Ohio Senate, has operated a public relations agency, and is a semi-retired tenured professor in political science. She has written mostly mysteries and thrillers since 1999.

The author is affiliated with the African Literature Association, the American Association of University Women, the Chanticleer Authors' Conference, the North Carolina Writers' Network, and the Women's National Book Association.

M. J.
SIMMS
MADDOX
Author